Fleet Air Arm Legends

FAIREY SWORDFISH

MATTHEW WILLIS

For Lieutenant Brian Edward Ryley RNVR, Légion d'Honneur (Chevalier), 1923–2021

Published in 2022 by Tempest Books
an imprint of Mortons Books Ltd.
Media Centre
Morton Way
Horncastle LN9 6JR
www.mortonsbooks.co.uk

Tempest Books

Copyright © Tempest Books, 2022
All rights reserved. No part of this publication may be reproduced or transmitted in any form or by any means, electronic or mechanical including photocopying, recording, or any information storage retrieval system without prior permission in writing from the publisher.
ISBN 978-1-911658-49-8

The right of Matthew Willis to be identified as the author of this work has been asserted in accordance with the Copyright, Designs and Patents Act 1988.

All images are courtesy the author unless otherwise stated.
Title page image courtesy of Menzies family.

Typeset by Jayne Clements (jayne@hinoki.co.uk), Hinoki Design and Typesetting

Acknowledgements: The author is indebted to former Swordfish aircrews Brian Ryley, Bertie Vigrass, Peter Jinks and Archie Hemsley; Paul Beaver, Philip Ryley, David McNaught, Margaret Sayer, Andreas Biermann, Peter Menzies and Mary Ann Bennett; Navy Wings, especially Katie Campbell, Louise Evans, Jon Parkinson and Jim Norris; Nick Hewitt of the National Museum of the RN; the BAE Systems Brough Heritage volunteers; and the reading room staff at The National Archives, Kew.

CONTENTS

Introduction: The End	7
1. The Beginning	8
2. The Swordfish is Born	12
3. To War	24
4. The Mediterranean	38
5. Triumph and Tragedy	51
6. Malta, the Red Sea and Crete	57
7. Sink the *Bismarck*!	65
8. Slaughter in the Channel	74
9. New Fronts	77
10. Battling the Wolfpacks	87
11. Defeating the U-boats	100
12. Day of Days	115
Notes	124
Data	127
Index	128

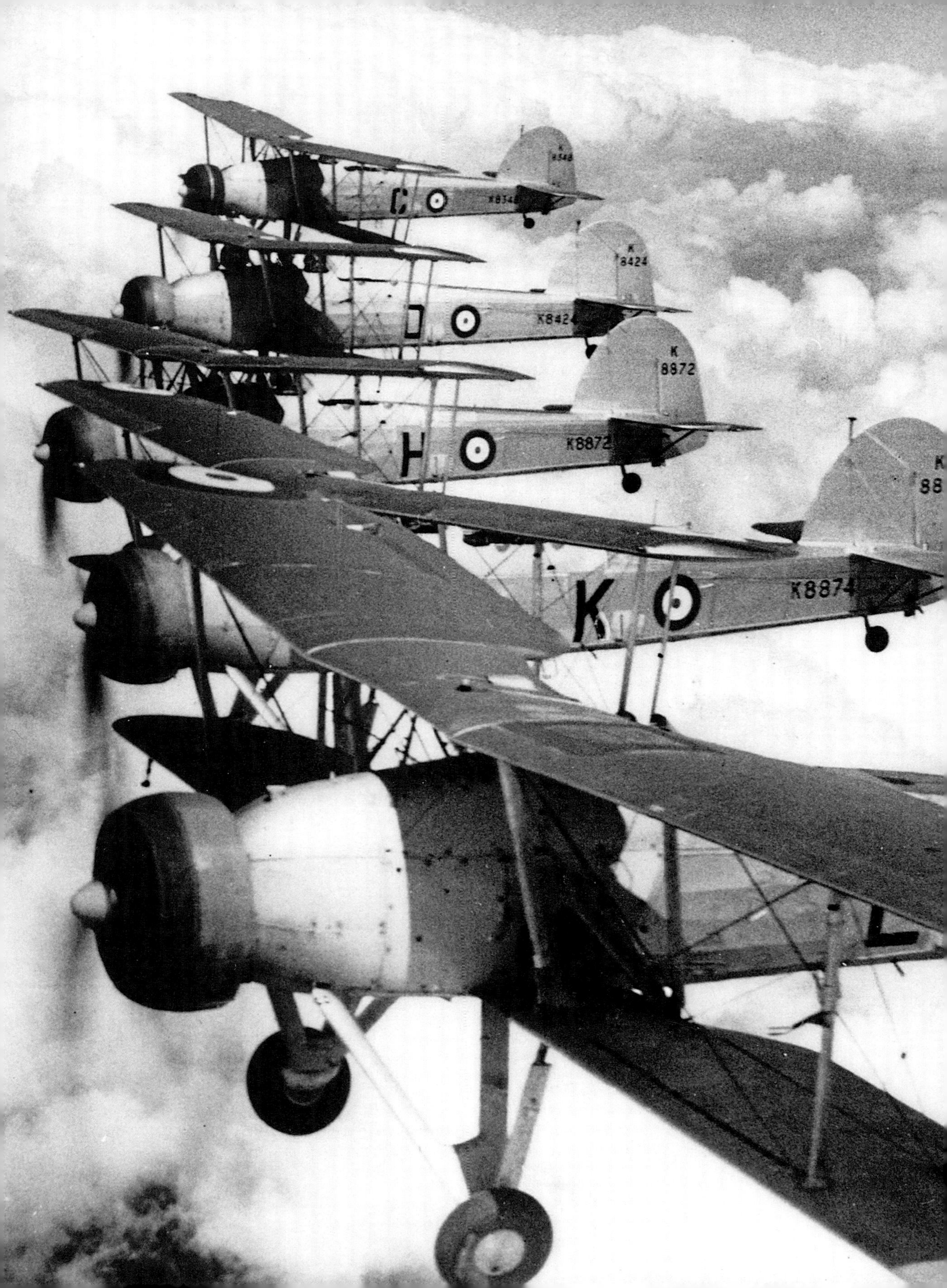
C
K
8424
D
K8424
K
8872
H
K8872
K
K8874
L

INTRODUCTION: THE END

IN AUGUST 1939, the Fleet Air Arm (FAA) was preparing for the end of the Fairey Swordfish. The biplane torpedo aircraft, bomber, gunnery spotter and reconnaissance aircraft had been in service for three years, and had proved popular and effective, but advances in aviation technology meant that it was quickly being surpassed. It was an open-cockpit, fabric-covered biplane in an era that belonged increasingly to sleek, stressed-skin monoplanes.

Manufacture of the type was due to end in November that year, by which time its successor, the Fairey Albacore, would be about to replace it on the production lines. The Albacore was still a biplane but significantly more modern, with a metal-skinned fuselage, fully enclosed cockpits and a newer, more powerful engine. It was still slow by modern standards, but had a useful increase in performance over the Swordfish. The aircraft expected to eclipse them both — a monoplane with far more advanced technology and performance — was on the drawing board and due in service in 1941.

The trouble was that the Admiralty now believed that war with Germany was inevitable and imminent — and probably at the worst possible time when it came to supply of aircraft. By September, Swordfish production would be running at 26 aircraft a month, but the switch to Albacore production would see deliveries fall to a mere two aircraft in December. Monthly deliveries would not be back in the twenties until July and would not rise appreciably above that for many more months. The Fleet Air Arm could easily run out of aircraft if wartime losses were as predicted.

There was a possible escape route, however. The Blackburn company had been approached to licence-build 400 Albacores in addition to those built by Fairey. If the Blackburn order for Albacores was changed to Swordfish, it would mean that the aircraft from that factory would be available four months earlier, as all the jigs and much of the tooling would already be available. It would not stop the immediate crisis but it might mean that by the time losses became critical, there would be enough new aircraft to plug the gap.

The Admiralty had a dilemma. It could switch to the more modern machine as planned, and go to war with the best possible capability in its torpedo squadrons, then and in the future — but risk severe shortages if losses mounted up. Alternatively, it could carry on with the Swordfish alongside the Albacore, in the knowledge that the aircraft was getting long in the tooth, but it would be more likely to keep numbers of aircraft up.

In reality, there was only one choice. The Fleet Air Arm would need more than double the supply of aircraft that were already being produced. Relying on a trickle of new aircraft for the foreseeable future was untenable. It was a numbers game, and the Swordfish represented better numbers. Newer aircraft were still needed in time, but in the meantime, the Swordfish would have to soldier on.

1

THE BEGINNING

IN 1930, the Fleet Air Arm of the Royal Air Force (RAF) – the British naval air service – had two main suppliers of aircraft. These were the Blackburn Aircraft Company and Fairey Aviation. The latter had supplied fighters, bombers and reconnaissance aircraft to the FAA since the end of the First World War, but Blackburn had a lockout on the provision of torpedo aircraft since 1923. The torpedo was the main weapon to achieve what the Fleet Air Arm was designed to do – damage and disable the ships of an enemy battle fleet, which was only possible with sub-surface running, self-propelled explosive projectiles. The other classes of aircraft were effectively there to facilitate the torpedo aircraft or the ships of the fleet. Fairey was not prepared to let its rival do all the running in this regard.

In March 1928, the Air Ministry and Admiralty put a specification out to the industry for a torpedo aircraft. In fact, a new aircraft had only just been ordered – the Blackburn Ripon Mk II was an improvement of an earlier prototype built to a 1923 requirement. Although the Ripon II was initially considered an interim type, it would in fact go on to equip the Fleet Air Arm into the late 1930s (its life extended by a couple of years by the addition of a new air-cooled engine and a new name, the Baffin). Nevertheless, a new specification was Specification M.5/28 was for a 'two-seater torpedo carrying ship-plane' with a performance somewhat better than the Ripon and which could carry the new 18in Mk X torpedo. Submissions were received from Handley-Page, Blackburn and Fairey.

Fairey's design was a large, conventional biplane with broad-chord, slightly swept wings with rounded tips. It was to be powered by a Rolls-Royce F.10 engine (which would later become the Kestrel) and was designed to carry the streamline-body Mk X torpedo partially recessed within the fuselage. Specification M.5/28 was, however, cancelled in January 1930 and a new specification, M.1/30, issued. One factor was the end of production of the Mk X torpedo, amid a short-lived period in which the Royal Navy (RN) began to move to a larger, heavier, aerial torpedo. The development of a new weapon weighing up to 1,900lb had been initiated in 1928 and was known as the Type K. This emerged as a torpedo with an overall weight of 1,866lb and 700lb of explosive, more than double the 320lb of the earlier Mk VIII torpedo, but at the expense of a longer range.

Fairey was one of five companies to submit a proposal, presumably with a developed version of its M.5/28 design, although no details are available for its later submission. Once again, the specification was cancelled (this time the Air Ministry had decided that aerial torpedoes need not weigh more than 1,500lb, so the larger aircraft was not needed) but not before prototypes were ordered from three companies — Fairey not among them. The M.1/30A contenders would go on to undergo rather leisurely testing. An aircraft derived from Blackburn's design evolved into the B-6, which received an order from the Fleet Air Arm as the Shark, and would go on to enter squadron service in 1935.

It seemed that Fairey would once again miss out on the chance to supply the Fleet Air Arm with a torpedo aircraft. Another specification issued in 1930, however, was for a replacement for the Fairey's venerable III/Seal family in Fleet Air Arm service (S.9/30). The role of this aircraft would be reconnaissance, and directing (or 'spotting') the fall of shot of the Royal Navy's big-gun warships. They also had a subsidiary role as light bombers, carrying small bombs on carriers beneath the wings.

As Blackburn had been virtually the sole supplier of torpedo aircraft to the FAA since 1923, Fairey had had a similar near-monopoly with spotter/reconnaissance aircraft since 1924. The company therefore had a good chance of its own aircraft being successful. There was stiff competition, however — six companies prepared designs, though in the end not all of them made submissions. Fairey did so in October, and was rewarded with an order for a prototype. The Fairey S.9/30, developed under chief designer Marcel Lobelle, represented a break from the tried-and-tested layout of the III series, with its long, unswept and unstaggered two-bay wings. Arguably, the S.9/30 owed more to the M.5/28 torpedo aircraft, with wings in particular of a very similar planform — single bay, staggered, and slightly swept, with a shorter span and greater chord than Fairey's previous spotter-reconnaissance types. In common with most Fleet Air Arm types, the S.9/30 was required to be convertible from a landplane (i.e. with a wheeled undercarriage, even if it was to operate mainly from a carrier deck) to a floatplane. The crew would be three-strong — a pilot, an observer (the Fleet Air Arm term for a specialist navigator) and a radio operator, who would also operate the defensive guns (a Telegraphist Air Gunner, or TAG in FAA parlance). To power the S.9/30, Fairey chose the 525hp Rolls-Royce Kestrel IIMS, a liquid-cooled V12 engine that used partial steam-cooling to reduce the size of radiators needed and therefore cut aerodynamic drag.

Around this time, Fairey became aware of a requirement by the Greek Navy for a general-purpose aircraft that would be capable of torpedo attack as well as reconnaissance. The company judged that an adaptation of its S.9/30 design would be suitable, and set about building a prototype as a private venture, which was simply known in the company as the 'Greek Machine'. The airframe appeared to be in most respects identical to that of the S.9/30, with a few detail differences, but was powered by an air-cooled radial engine. Interestingly, when the S.9/30 appeared, it had a split undercarriage suitable for torpedo carriage. Fairey informed the Admiralty about this aircraft, when progress on the prototype was only few months behind the S.9/30. One story suggests that Sir Richard Fairey told the 'chiefs of the FAA' that the S.9/30 was "ten times more expensive to build than the private-venture 'Greek machine' ... [which] could do everything that the S.9/30 could do".[1] This is somewhat hard to credit, as the aircraft was virtually identical apart from the engine installation and the former's ability to carry a torpedo. However it happened the Admiralty immediately showed interest in the 'Greek Machine', with the result that Fairey accelerated work on it, and the private venture type first flew almost a year before the 'official' one.

A likely reason for this was a change in doctrine in the Fleet Air Arm. In 1930, the service responded to financial pressures and the constraints placed on it by the Air Ministry by seeking to share its

The Fairey TSR (construction number F1875) as it first flew on 21 March 1933 from Great West Aerodrome in the hands of Chris Staniland, powered by an Armstrong Siddeley Panther.

roles across fewer aircraft types. The FAA had previously considered that at least three aircraft types in service at any one time were necessary to cover the roles of torpedo attack, reconnaissance, gunnery spotting, escort of strike/reconnaissance missions, and fleet defence (with either float or wheel undercarriage). A proposal from Fleet Air Arm officers suggested reducing this to two. The torpedo strike and spotter roles were to be combined into a three-seater type, known as a Torpedo-Spotter-Reconnaissance aircraft, or TSR. Escort and fleet defence would be provided by a two-seat fighter, with reconnaissance able to be carried out by both types.

This was naturally not without complications. The spotter-reconnaissance was typically a three-seat aircraft, while the specialist torpedo aircraft only required two crew. However, the 1930 decision that 1,500lb was adequate for aerial torpedoes freed up 500lb of weight-carrying requirement, meaning a smaller and lighter aircraft than the M.1/30 contenders could fulfil the specification and still leave scope for a third crew member and his equipment.

This led to yet another new specification, the third in five years for a new torpedo aircraft. The previous requirement, M.1/30, was cancelled along with the spotter-reconnaissance specification S.9/30 and a new, combined and amended requirement issued in the form of S.15/33. This time, the offensive load was reduced to a 1,500lb torpedo or equivalent in bombs, but with a similar performance. Interestingly, the top speed called for in S.15./33 was slightly slower than that specified in M.5/28 fully five years earlier, although the failure of any of the prototypes from the earlier competitions to meet their performance targets might have convinced the Air Ministry that there was no point asking for more. As it happened, the S.15/33 contenders would miss even the modest performance set out in the specification. At this point, the Admiralty was intent on acquiring an aircraft that could do all the tasks required of it more than it was on out-and-out performance while doing them, which often put it in conflict with the Air Ministry, which tended to favour performance over capability.

The 'Greek Machine' first flew on 21 March 1933 at Harmondsworth aerodrome, piloted by the company's chief test pilot Chris Staniland. As completed, it was powered by a 625hp Armstrong Siddeley Panther VI, which appears to have been the engine preferred by the Greek Navy, but within a few months it was replaced by a Bristol Pegasus. On 10 July the revised aircraft first flew with the new engine and wheel spats fitted. From this point, the aircraft was known as the Fairey TSR. Trials continued and were apparently promising, until 11 September, when Staniland made a flight to assess spin performance with the automatic leading-edge slats unlocked. The TSR was extremely stable and it proved difficult to induce a spin. This was not unusual in aircraft of this configuration — the competing Blackburn Shark was also extremely difficult to spin. Unfortunately, when Staniland finally managed to encourage the TSR to enter a spin, the aircraft's attitude immediately became very flat and the rotation fast, and none of the usual actions to return to controlled flight proved effective. After 12 revolutions, Staniland felt he had no choice but to bail out, which he did safely, but the TSR was destroyed in the resulting crash.

Things looked bleak for Fairey. There had only been one prototype, and there was no second machine under construction to carry on the programme. Meanwhile Blackburn had produced a completely revised version of its M.1/30 design, and its S.15/33 contender based on this design (later to become the Shark) was nearing completion. Gloster had modified its FS.36 design (FS for 'fleet spotter') into the TSR.38, and the aircraft had been flying in that form for two months. By the time it would customarily take to produce a second TSR, the Admiralty and Air Ministry would most likely have already made a decision. And before that, changes would have to be made to the design to ensure the irrecoverable flat spin would not recur. What followed demonstrated the company's determination and belief in its aircraft.

2

THE SWORDFISH IS BORN

Work was immediately started on a second prototype, with amendments to ensure better response in a spin. These included lengthening the rear fuselage by some four feet, enlarging the vertical tail surfaces, and adding strakes to the rear fuselage to ensure airflow was directed over the rudder during a spin. The wing planform was also adjusted, with the lower wing no longer swept, and the upper wing area and shape altered slightly thanks to the leading edge being squared off at the tip, which also allowed for the anti-stall slats to be lengthened and extended almost to the tip. The Townend ring around the circumference of the engine was of broader chord, and incorporated an exhaust collector ring in the leading edge. This revised design was designated TSR II.

According to H.A. Taylor, "By giving top priority to the project and cutting right across normal works procedures – so that assemblies were made in any convenient part of the factory as the drawings came through – the TSR II, prototype for the Swordfish, was completed and flown in seven months."[2]

The first flight of the new machine was made on 17 April 1934 – a remarkable turnaround, which effectively kept Fairey in the competition alongside Blackburn and Gloster.

Contractor's trials were carried out by Fairey until June, when the aircraft was passed to the Aeroplane and Armament Experimental Establishment (A&AEE) for initial tests, by which time it had been allocated the serial K4190. These tests were necessarily brief, as catapult tests at RAE Farnborough and deck-landing trials aboard HMS *Courageous* had to be fitted in. The TSR II returned to Martlesham for more extensive A&AEE trials in August, Flight Lieutenant Duncan Menzies picking up the aircraft from Hayes on 3 August 1934. By now, all three TSR competitors were at Martlesham, and the test pilots there were able to assess them back-to-back.

Other than a few handling niggles, the Fairey showed up well. Fortunately, the changes made to the design after the loss of the first TSR were effective, and recovery from spins could be effected quickly and easily. The aircraft left Martlesham in October 1934 while the Blackburn and Gloster continued testing there, but the A&AEE report was not completed until April 1935. The report must have been well received as an order for three more prototypes and a production batch of 86 aircraft was placed shortly afterwards. To put this in perspective, the Blackburn Shark received an initial production order of just 16 aircraft (and even the second production batch was only for

The prototype Fairey TSR II as it was originally rolled out in May 1934, with a two-blade propeller, a Townend ring with bulges over the cylinder heads, and prominent anti-spin strakes on the rear fuselage, and as fitted with float undercarriage operating off the Hamble in November that year. (AUTHOR AND MENZIES FAMILY)

K4190 as modified in 1935 with a smooth Townend ring and three-blade propeller of production standard.

53 machines). Both the Blackburn and the Fairey had proved superior to the Gloster, which did not proceed beyond prototype stage.

On acceptance by the Air Ministry, the TSR II received the formal name 'Swordfish'. (The naming policy for Fleet Air Arm aircraft at the time was for TSRs to be named after predatory fish, and for fighters to be named after seabirds.) An order for a second, even larger, batch of 104 aircraft was placed in 1935, with 150 more ordered two years later, by which time the Swordfish was the sole torpedo bomber in FAA service.

The first of the three pre-production aircraft, K5660, was completed in December 1935; K5661 and K5662 followed in January 1936. One of the first people to fly these aircraft was Flight Lieutenant Menzies, who had been heavily involved in the A&AEE trials on the three TSR aircraft, but had moved to Fairey Aviation in the meantime. His logbooks show the extent of manufacturers' trials of the first three production-spec Swordfish as they became available over the first few months of 1936 from Great West Aerodrome, joined occasionally by K4190. Particular attention during this phase was paid to the ailerons, which were light and effective at all speeds but had a tendency to snatch during the stall. The ailerons could be drooped to provide something of the effect of a wing flap, but in reality, this was barely effective and rarely used. General handling was still being addressed, as was lateral and longitudinal stability (the Martlesham tests had indicated some instability in the dive with the centre of gravity near the aft limit). 'Flettner strips' (a projecting strip along the trailing edges of a control surface) were tested on ailerons and elevators in an effort to perfect control. The anti-spin strakes evidently turned out to be unnecessary, and they did not appear on production aircraft.

In March, K5662 was fitted as a floatplane, and company testing moved to Southampton Water. Meanwhile, early production aircraft began to

The last of three pre-production Swordfish K5662s, completed with floats, taking part in tests on Southampton Water with Fairey test pilot Duncan Menzies in 1936. (MENZIES FAMILY)

appear in February and undergo testing at Great West before delivery to the service.

Testing on with floats did not proceed as satisfactorily as the version with wheeled undercarriage, and in truth as a floatplane, the Swordfish was never entirely satisfactory. Manoeuvrability at low speed was inadequate, the water rudders never met the turning circle requirement and the floats could take a long time to get up onto the steps, during which time the propeller would be pounded with damaging spray. Even when the aircraft had ridden up onto the steps of the floats, the ride was rough and uncomfortable, and the pilot had to take care that the aircraft was not bounced into the air before it reached flying speed. In the air, handling of the floatplane Swordfish was better, but overall, the aircraft was less satisfactory as a floatplane than as a landplane.

When the first Swordfish were delivered to the Fleet Air Arm in July 1936, its competitor, the Blackburn Shark, had been in service for 18 months. This was not a happy period, as persistent reliability niggles with the Shark's engines and oil system had prevented the FAA from making full use of its new aircraft.

The TSRs were replacing two distinct classes of aircraft, the Fairey IIIF and Seal spotter-reconnaissance, and the Blackburn Baffin torpedo bomber. The first unit to convert to the Swordfish, 825 Naval Air Squadron (NAS), had been a IIIF squadron (the oldest type, and hence most overdue for replacement), while the next two, 811 and 812 NAS, which converted in October and December 1936, had operated the Baffin. In October, 825 Squadron embarked on HMS *Glorious* for service in the Mediterranean, and switched between the carrier, Hal Far on Malta and Dekheila and Aboukir in Egypt for most of the next two years. The exception was a brief return home to take part in the Coronation Review of the fleet at Spithead to mark the ascension of George VI to the throne. Also participating were 811 and 812 Squadrons.

Early production Swordfish K5933 demonstrating the colour scheme early aircraft were delivered in, with silver dope on fabric surfaces, and 'Cerrux Grey' on most metal panels.

K5932 '73' and other aircraft of 812 Squadron over the assembled ships of the Royal Navy during the 1937 Fleet Review at Spithead, belatedly marking the coronation of King George VI.

The review itself was affected by poor weather, and mist and cloud made assembling the massive formation difficult. The aircraft were meant to fly past the Royal Yacht in squadron formation, diving to salute the Royal Yacht, before moving into wing formation and once again passing the warships. Because of the weather, the squadron formation and salute were dispensed with. The poor visibility hampered proceedings, but over a million people still turned out to see the review, and the sight of the Fleet Air Arm was unquestionably impressive. The next time a full, public fleet review would take place was in 1953; the 1937 event marked both the high point of the pre-war, all-biplane Fleet Air Arm and the beginning of its formation into a wartime service.

Although three of the squadrons taking part that day were flying Sharks, within two months they, too, would be operating Swordfish. From September 1937, the Swordfish was the sole TSR type in operation with the FAA. With the Albacore still on the drawing board at that time, the Swordfish was set to be the warhorse on which the FAA's strike force would train and organise for war against a powerful, well-equipped peer nation, evolving from the colonial police force it had been in the 1920s.

When the Swordfish was developed, and the main production orders placed, there was little immediate prospect of a global war, despite the increased tensions resulting from the rise of Nazi Germany. The brief panic over a possible British retaliation to the Italian invasion of Ethiopia in 1935/6 had not changed policy with regard to rearmament, and the usual peacetime process of a new specification every few years to replace existing types with newer ones continued. It was commonplace for a new specification to be issued more or less as the previous type was coming into service, and this was no exception with the

The first frontline Fleet Air Arm unit to equip with Swordfish was 825 Squadron, of HMS *Glorious*' air group, indicated by the diagonal yellow band on the rear fuselage, flying in Vics of three. The squadron wore three-digit side numbers from 967 to 981 between July 1936 and May 1939.

Swordfish. Specification M.7/36 was raised in 1936, which led to the Fairey Albacore, the type that was intended to replace the Swordfish and Shark (although the Shark would be withdrawn from frontline use in 1937 following persistent problems with its oil system). The Albacore was expected to be a short-lived, interim design, given the rapid advances in aviation technology, so yet another specification, S.24/37, was raised the following year, calling for a much more advanced TSR with considerably better performance. Within two years of that specification, it was expected that the Swordfish would have been replaced by the Albacore, and by 1941, the S.24/37 monoplane would be coming into service.

This expectation did not seriously change until 1939, when the possibility of war became a near-inevitability. It was not until August that the Admiralty took serious steps to build up production, though many of the Admiralty's requirements were resisted by the Air Ministry. The last order for the Swordfish was due to be completed in November that year, with the Albacore taking over the following month, reaching a production level of 20 TSR aircraft a month by July 1940. This meant a dip in deliveries to the FAA at the worst possible time – 26 aircraft (Swordfish) in November 1939, falling to just two aircraft (Albacores) in December, deliveries failing to reach previous levels for eight months. This would have been manageable in peacetime, but was totally inadequate for a war which it was expected might start in October. (As it turned out, war would be declared a month earlier than that.) The Admiralty assessed that it would need 50 TSRs a month to keep up with wartime loss rates. If wartime rates were to be achieved, a rate of 35 aircraft a month would have to be attained while peace continued to hold. The head of Air Branch at the Admiralty wrote in a memorandum of 28 August 1939, "If factory extensions are necessary, it might be worth taking steps to increase the production of Albacores as

A Swordfish of 825 Squadron runs up at RAF Hal Far, Malta in 1936, shortly after the squadron replaced its Fairey IIIFs for service in the Mediterranean Fleet.

it is understood this machine is preferred to the Swordfish." The only way to maintain the level of aircraft needed was to keep the Swordfish in production while the Albacore began. This would mean either enlarging the Fairey factory at Hayes, or finding production capacity somewhere else.

Duly, an order was discussed with Blackburn to build 400 Albacores, with Admiralty assistance given to the company to set up a factory at Sherburn in Elmet, near Leeds, where Blackburn had a presence with their flying school, with the added advantage that it was close to Blackburn's Olympia works. The factory buildings, to Ministry of Aircraft production designs, were commissioned quickly, and arrangements made for around 60% of the work to be sub-contracted to local companies.

However, when war broke out in September, the production arrangements were still inadequate to meet the Fleet Air Arm's needs. With agreement from Blackburn and support from Fairey, the Admiralty sought permission from the Treasury to switch the proposed order for Albacores to Swordfish:

> The performance of the Swordfish is substantially inferior to that of the Albacore in several respects, but the Admiralty have come to the conclusion these disadvantages would be outweighed by the prospective acceleration in output to meet the anticipated deficiencies of the Fleet Air Arm in this important type of aircraft.

At this point, the Admiralty thought it would begin to receive the Albacore replacement, the S.24/37 Barracuda, from March 1941 — in fact, for various reasons, deliveries of the later type would not begin until late 1942.

The crucial advantage of Blackburn building the Swordfish would be that most of the existing jigs and tools for the Hayes production line could

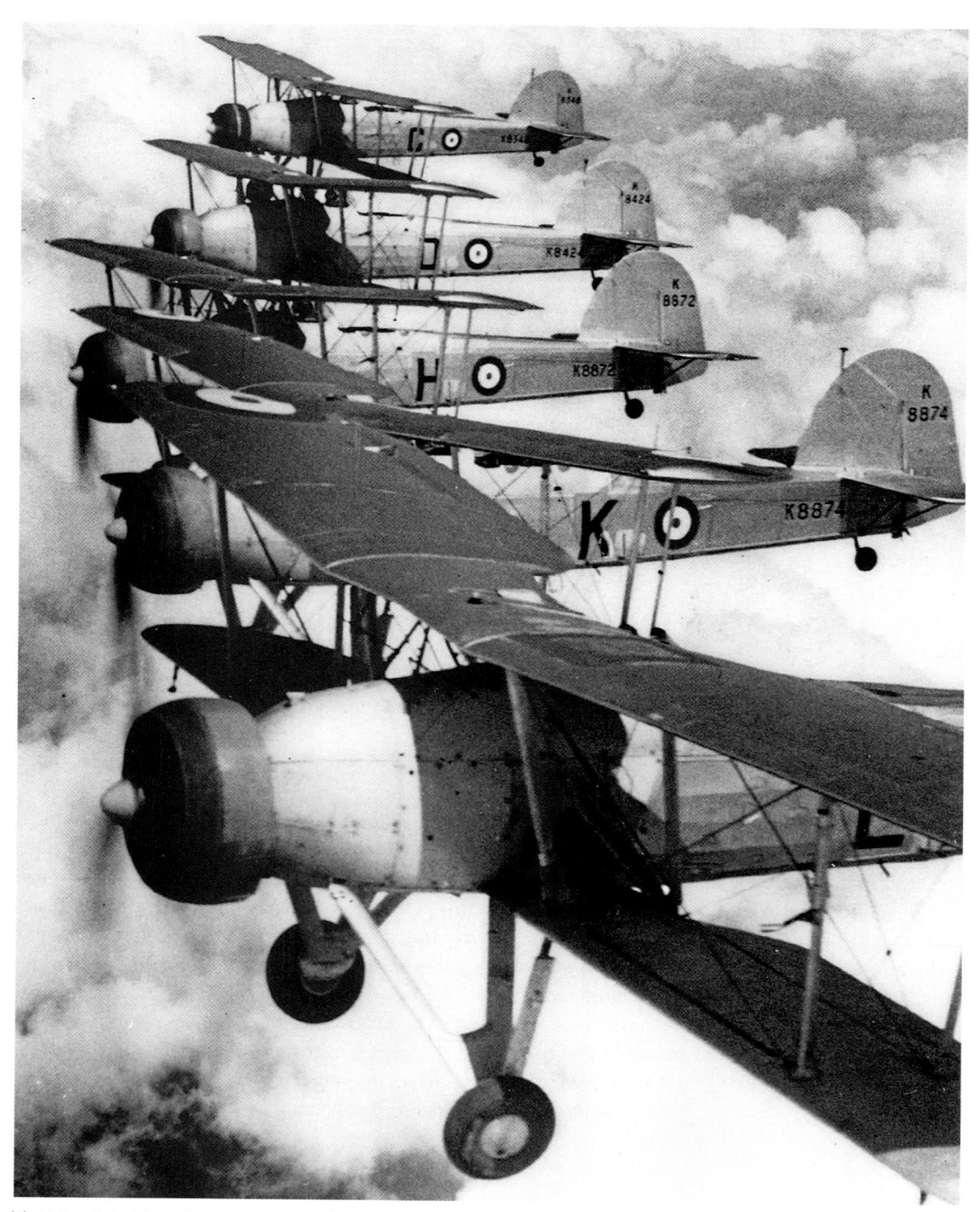

'A' Flight of the Torpedo Training Unit (TTU), based at RAF Gosport for training aircrews using the range in Stokes Bay. These aircraft were from the second production batch.

K8426 '6' from 'A' Flight TTU, demonstrating an imperfect torpedo drop with a practice projectile, 1938/9.

be transferred to Sherburn, drastically short-cutting the time Blackburn would need to tool up. If Blackburn were to build Albacores in parallel with Fairey, it would mean starting from scratch. The Fleet Air Arm gambled that receiving an older aircraft sooner would be better than a newer one later. It was this decision that secured the future of the aircraft. Without it, the Swordfish could not conceivably have continued in frontline roles much after 1941. As it was, the Swordfish served the Royal Navy until the end of the war and beyond.

At the outbreak of war, 13 frontline squadrons were equipped with the Swordfish. By 1938, all of the 'legacy' types — IIIFs, Seals and Baffins — had been replaced, as well as Sharks of 810, 820, 821 and 822 Squadrons. The Admiralty considered, however, that "The types of aircraft in service with the Fleet Air Arm were obsolete."[3] If anything, the situation with carriers was worse; the RN had six that were suitable for frontline operations, none of which was armoured, and only one (*Ark Royal*) was truly modern. Newer carriers were under construction, all of which had substantial armour protection, the first (HMS *Illustrious*) due to commission in April 1940, and the second (*Formidable*) in October.

Three images of Fairey Swordfish floatplanes of HMS *Glorious*' air group, October 1937. K5957 '72' of 812 Squadron is craned over the side, K8351 '810' of 823 Squadron is prepared on the quarterdeck and '809' has its wheel chassis changed for floats, overseen by the ship's cat.

A Vic of Swordfish from 822 NAS, HMS *Furious*, demonstrating the colourful markings that were typical of the Fleet Air Arm in the late 1930s, including a black upper deck and chequered pattern on the upper wing and tail surfaces of '907', indicating a flight leader's aircraft. Fuselage bands were red.

3

TO WAR

As soon as war broke out, the RN's carriers were almost entirely occupied with hunting for German surface raiders and protecting trade routes from them, and in offensive anti-submarine operations. HMS *Glorious* sailed through the Suez Canal and patrolled in the Indian Ocean for enemy raiders and merchantmen. This turned out to be an uneventful period for ship and aircrews, 812 and 825 Squadrons not disembarking until January when the carrier returned to Malta in January 1940 for a refit.

The early days of war had seen U-boats taking advantage of the rich pickings in the Western Approaches. The Admiralty hurriedly responded with submarine-hunting groups to patrol the seas to the south and west of Britain in the hope of deterring the attacks. The groups, which consisted of a carrier and an escort of four destroyers, were to be dispatched into the area where U-boats had been operating in an attempt to drive them away. The idea was that the carrier's aircraft would patrol, forcing any U-boats to submerge, while the destroyer escort would use their Asdic (sonar) to pinpoint the craft and attack with depth charges.

This was not the work that the FAA's TSR squadrons had expected to do on the outbreak of war. It was an untried strategy and would soon prove disastrous. HMS *Ark Royal* left Scapa Flow on 11 September. Three days later, lookouts spotted torpedo tracks, but the torpedoes detonated short of the carrier. The escorting destroyers immediately went on the attack, and a depth charge brought *U-39* to the surface. Despite this near-miss, when *Ark Royal* returned, HMS *Courageous*, with her Swordfish of 811 and 822 Squadrons, put to sea from Plymouth on 16 September. The following day, a distress call was picked up from the merchantman SS *Kafiristan,* under attack from a U-boat about 350 miles west of Cape Clear on the southern tip of Ireland. Four Swordfish were launched and two of the destroyers detached to the scene of the attack. When they reached the vicinity, one of the Swordfish forced the submarine (*U-53*) to submerge at about 1700, but by this time, the *Kafiristan* had already been sunk.

Unbeknownst to *Courageous*, another U-boat was in the vicinity; *U-29* sighted the carrier and her two remaining escorts at 1800. The carrier was not flying a local patrol, and all aircraft that were airborne had been searching for *U-53*, many miles distant. The submarine stalked the carrier but was unable to manoeuvre into a favourable position. Until, that was, the four aircraft that had flown off to investigate *Kafiristan*'s report returned. *Courageous* turned into wind and recovered the Swordfish, unwittingly turning directly towards *U-29*. At

A poor-quality but important image of a Swordfish in action a few weeks into the Second World War. SS *American Farmer* was picking up 29 crewmembers in lifeboats from SS *Kafiristan*, which had been torpedoed in the Atlantic by U-53, on 17 September 1939. The submarine was nearby, her captain having waited to ensure the survivors were rescued, but as the rescue was taking place, a Swordfish from HMS *Courageous* appeared and bombed the U-boat, forcing it to dive. Passenger W.A. Hamilton of Toledo, Ohio, took this photograph as the Swordfish attacked.

1950, the submarine fired three torpedoes, two of which struck *Courageous*, which almost immediately began to list, and sank in just 17 minutes.

The loss was a heavy blow for the Fleet Air Arm, as not only did it remove one of the few large fleet carriers (apart from *Ark Royal*, *Courageous* and her sister *Glorious* were the two most capable carriers in the RN at the time), but two full squadrons of Swordfish. None of the squadrons' air crew were among the 516 killed, but many Fleet Air Arm and RAF maintenance personnel lost their lives. (The RAF was still providing personnel at this stage, while the FAA built up its own pool of maintainers.)

The destruction of two full squadrons of aircraft in one blow was serious for the FAA, as supplies of replacement Swordfish would stop in November and not recommence until the Blackburn production line was up and running, whenever that might be. In order to expedite production at Sherburn in Elmet after the Hayes factory switched to Albacores, Fairey transferred all jigs and tools that were specific to the Swordfish to Blackburn. They also asked the 100 or so subcontractors who had produced components to sell the tools to Blackburn.

Even so, the last Fairey-built Swordfish rolled off the production line at Hayes on 30 November 1939, and the first Blackburn-built machine only flew in December 1940. Blackburn still needed to source materials for production — easier said than done under wartime conditions. One of the benefits of

Swordfish L7682 'A2A' of 810 Squadron burning after a crash on *Ark Royal* in May 1939. In the first image a firefighter in an asbestos suit hurries to the wreck; in the second, deck crew with hoses attempt to extinguish the fire. The crew escaped unharmed.

switching the order of 400 Albacores to Swordfish was that, according to the Admiralty in a memo to the Treasury, "the materials for the Swordfish could be supplied more readily; the quantity of light alloy used in the Swordfish being less than in the Albacore".[4] Indeed, use of light alloys was mostly confined to the wing and tail ribs, with some alloy cowling panels and other small items. The Albacore had a semi-monocoque fuselage with a light alloy skin. Even so, certain metal forgings and stampings were in high demand, together with other materials such as duralumin bars, and Blackburn was at the back of the queue.

Furthermore, Fairey had retained all the tools that were used for parts on its other types as well as the Swordfish, so Blackburn did not receive a full set of tools from the parent company and needed to have enough of those manufactured for the production line's needs. Fairey helped by supplying a few sets along with drawings, and four staff members with knowledge of the processes were transferred to Blackburn. Two pattern aircraft were delivered — P4254 was received at Sherburn on 26 October 1939 and P4232 in April 1940 — one of them totally dismantled and rebuilt, and known in the company as the 'Fairey Godmother'. Both would rejoin the Fleet Air Arm and have long and varied careers.

Despite the rapid moves to establish a new source of Swordfish, the Fleet Air Arm had to conduct virtually the first year of the war with no replacements other than the reserves it had built up before November 1939.

Meanwhile, carriers had been withdrawn from anti-submarine operations in the Western Approaches. Not only had *Courageous* been lost, but *Ark Royal* had only just avoided suffering a similar fate, so it was clear that these operations were far too risky. With the destroyer escort in place and aircraft patrolling, it should have been virtually impossible for a U-boat to pose a threat, but, as the 17 September incident showed, circumstances meant that it was not always possible to keep the screen in place. For the Fleet Air Arm, it proved to be a very costly failed experiment. The 'hunter-killer' group did not prove workable until later in the war, with better equipment and technology, not to mention more plentiful (and expendable) escort carriers.

After *Ark Royal*'s narrow escape, she was dispatched south to join the hunt for raiders with Force K. Protecting trade routes from surface raiders was something the RN was much better prepared for than submarine hunting. In 1938, the RN's 'Air requirements for war' had been formulated, which concluded that while an aircraft carrier cost the same as three 8,000-ton cruisers, its aircraft could search an area that would require 25 surface ships. The committee considered "a well-balanced force to take action on the trade routes against an enemy raider would be composed of three cruisers and one carrier".[5]

In the latter part of 1939, most of the RN carrier force was occupied in this task. Six mixed task groups plied the oceans — in the Atlantic was HMS *Glorious* with the battleships *Warspite* and *Malaya*, *Argus* with *Queen Elizabeth*, *Furious* with the battle-cruiser *Repulse*, *Hermes* with the French battle-cruiser *Strasbourg*, and *Ark Royal* with the battle-cruiser *Renown* and cruiser *Neptune*, while in the Indian Ocean was *Eagle* with cruisers *Cornwall* and *Gloucester*.

The carriers had no success locating enemy raiders, and were little better at finding enemy merchant ships. They did, however, at least help narrow down the areas that raiders could hide in, and the Admiralty believed that the presence of carriers was confining raiders to "operations of minor importance".[6] On 22 November, Force K, the group including *Ark Royal* (carrying 810 and 821 Squadrons) located the German liner *Adolph Woermann*, whose crew promptly scuttled it. Unbeknownst to Force K, the raider *Graf Spee* was then re-entering the South Atlantic from the Indian Ocean, and on 25 November, passed within a couple of hundred miles of the task group, not

L7672 'A7F' and other aircraft of 820 Squadron, HMS *Ark Royal*'s air group, over the south coast of England in 1939. The three-character alphanumeric codes were adopted in May that year, with the first letter indicating the carrier, the number indicating the squadron and the final letter denoting the individual aircraft. The air group fuselage band is blue-red-blue.

too far outside the Swordfish's patrol radius. On that day, the crews took part in torpedo attack practice, little knowing how close they had come to the real thing. A week later, they received a distress signal from the *Doric Star* under attack, 1,200 miles away off Walvis Bay, which would have taken three days to cover even if the ships were not by then short of fuel. *Ark Royal* could do nothing but put into Cape Town to refuel, while the Swordfish crews took the opportunity to fly their aircraft ashore to swing compasses. By the time Commodore Harwood's cruiser squadron (one of the small number of task groups in the region without a carrier) sighted the *Graf Spee*'s smoke on 13 December, Force K was 2,000 miles away to the north-east and again starting to run low on fuel.

They put into Rio de Janeiro for a rapid topping up of the bunkers, on the day that Captain Langsdorff made the decision to scuttle *Graf Spee* and save his crew. The Fleet Air Arm was again left to wait to see how its Swordfish would fare against a major Kriegsmarine warship.

Though this was still the period known as the 'phoney war', *Ark Royal* was at sea for 99 days of the 120 days between the commencement of hostilities and New Year 1940. Her aircraft had searched an estimated one million square miles in that time. After the destruction of the *Graf Spee*, the RN started to restore carriers to their normal stations, and *Glorious* passed through the Suez Canal back into the Mediterranean, while *Ark Royal* later joined her there via Gibraltar for

L2731 'A4G' of 820 Squadron, seen from another of the squadron's Swordfish, with a formation of the carrier's Blackburn Skua dive bomber-fighters in the background. This combination formed *Ark Royal*'s air group from 1938 to 1941.

exercises with her Swordfish, having left her Skuas at Hatston. *Furious* had already been withdrawn from the search to escort a convoy from Canada. This left *Eagle* searching for raiders in the Indian Ocean, while *Hermes* returned to the coast of West Africa after refitting in the UK.

Eagle's hunt for raiders was uneventful until 14 March when a 250lb bomb exploded in one of the rooms used for their storage. The resulting flash rushed through the bomb lift and into the hangar, burning the wing of one Swordfish. Two aircraft were hurriedly pulled out of the hangar, but the rest were doused with sea water when the hangar was sprayed to put the fire out. Despite this, all the aircraft were deemed fit to fly by the time the ship returned to Singapore for a much-needed refit.

Flying ceased after the explosion, but the next day the ship was able to fly off anti-submarine patrols. The Swordfish squadrons disembarked in May, and *Eagle* left Singapore for the Mediterranean.

*

On 3 April 1940, German forces initiated Operation *Weserübung*, the plan to occupy neutral Denmark and Norway. On 8 April, the loss of the destroyer HMS *Glowworm*, sunk off the Norwegian coast by the cruiser *Admiral Hipper*, revealed that something was afoot in Scandinavian waters. The carrier HMS *Furious* received orders to embark her squadrons rapidly – so much so that 801 Squadron was left behind at Evanton – and make for Norway. The absence of 801 Squadron's Skuas meant that

Blackburn-built Swordfish Mk I 'C1R' of 785 or 786 Squadron, RNAS Crail, in 1942/3, carrying an 18-inch dummy torpedo (Buoyant). One of several types of non-running torpedo for practice use, the Buoyant model was steel, while other types were concrete.

Furious' air group was effectively a Swordfish-only affair made up of 816 and 818 Squadrons. These had fortunately both been at Campbeltown and could rendezvous with *Furious* off the harbour there; 816 Squadron arrived promptly and landed on, though the wind changed and the visibility fell before 818 Squadron could find the carrier, and it took two hours of searching before the second Swordfish squadron could land. *Furious* then made her best speed to join three battleships and a cruiser squadron of the Home Fleet on the way to Trondheim, where German cruisers had been reported. In fact, the group was made up of the cruiser *Admiral Hipper* and the destroyers *Friedrich Eckoldt*, *Paul Jacobi*, *Bruno Heinemann* and *Theodor Riedel*, which had transported several divisions of mountain troops to the area.

Both Swordfish squadrons flew off early in the morning of 11 April armed with torpedoes, but *Admiral Hipper* had already left, escorted by *Friedrich Eckoldt*, leaving *Theodor Riedel, Paul Jacobi* and *Bruno Heinemann*. The aircraft of 816 Squadron attacked one of the destroyers, the *Theodor Riedel,* which they thought was anchored inshore, but had actually been beached on a sandbank to defend the harbour. The water was consequently too shallow for the torpedoes (most of which had been set to run at a depth suitable for a cruiser), and no hits were scored; 818 Squadron found another of the destroyers manoeuvring at speed, and made an attack despite the high ground nearby making the approach difficult. The commanding officer of HMS *Furious* reported that one hit might have been scored on the destroyer, but this seems unlikely. Lack of information had hampered the operation but the lesson had been learned, and an armed reconnaissance was flown back to the area later that day, the aircrews having orders to attack any enemy warships they saw after carrying out a thorough photographic study of the area. Each aircraft was armed with two 250lb and eight 20lb bombs — again, only a destroyer was seen (probably the *Paul Jacobi*), and attacked but all the bombs missed. Regular reconnaissance flights would be carried out from hereon in.

At this point, *Furious* was the only carrier in Norwegian waters. *Glorious* and *Ark Royal* would soon be dispatched from the Mediterranean, but for the first few days, the RN's oldest carrier and its Swordfish squadrons had to hold the line. The lack of fighters — even the flawed Skuas and outdated Sea Gladiators — limited *Furious* to operations in the north, out of range of enemy fighters, but the aircrews of 816 and 818 were still keen to prove what they and their aircraft were capable of.

On the morning of 12 April, the fleet arrived off Vestfjord (a large open body of water bounded by the Lofoten Islands and coast of the mainland) in the hope of attacking the Kriegsmarine destroyers bottled up there after the inconclusive First Battle of Narvik. In the afternoon, despite poor weather and appalling visibility, both squadrons flew off, 818 Squadron leading 816 by 40 minutes. According to Captain T.H. Troubridge, the officer commanding HMS *Furious*, "818 Squadron got through and delivered a dashing attack from low altitude". It was a nerve-wracking episode for the crews, attempting to pick their way through the mountains, whose tops were well into the cloud, but as they were lining up to attack, the murk lifted slightly and exposed the Swordfish to the combined mass of anti-aircraft fire from the assembled ships and guns recently installed on the shore. At least three hits are believed to have been scored on the destroyers with 250lb bombs, but two of the Swordfish were hit by the barrage, including the aircraft of 818 Squadron's CO, Lieutenant-Commander P.G.O. Sydney-Turner, and forced to ditch, while another Swordfish was damaged and the crew wounded. Further out to sea, the weather had worsened, and 816 Squadron found that the cloud was so low they could not identify landmarks to find the target. By this time, it would have been impossible to carry out a successful attack even if the Swordfish had managed to find their way to Narvik, so the leader decided to return to the carrier. This was easier said than done in the dense and low cloud with flurries of snow ever more intense. Troubridge risked switching searchlights on and shining them in the direction the Swordfish were expected to appear from, and this finally allowed the frozen and no doubt extremely relieved crews of 816 Squadron to land on. Nevertheless, *Furious* was pitching badly and Lt Donati swung on landing, his aircraft going over the side, parting the arrester wire the hook had caught. Fortunately, both he and his TAG were picked up by a destroyer.

It had been a brave and well-executed attack in extremely difficult conditions, and while little had been achieved on this occasion, being attacked from the air in such conditions would have done little good to the morale of the German destroyer crews. The Swordfish's ability to operate in weather that would ground many aircraft was already clear as a benefit of a type many in the service felt was already obsolete. Unfortunately, the losses from combat and accidents on 12 April had reduced the number of aircraft available for a strike to thirteen. All aircraft available were needed the following day, when the task force planned to deal decisively with the trapped destroyers in Operation *DW*, later known as the Second Battle of Narvik.

In addition to the aircraft with HMS *Furious*, the battleship HMS *Warspite* carried a floatplane Swordfish of 700 Squadron on her catapult. This was flown on the day of the operation by Petty Officer F.C. Rice and his observer Lieutenant-Commander W.L.M. Brown. As *Warspite* and her escorting destroyers approached Ofotfjord, where the Kriegsmarine ships lurked, Rice and Brown flew ahead, reporting the location of the

Swordfish floatplane P4199 'E8F' of 702 Squadron, the catapult aircraft of the battleship HMS *Resolution*, visits *Ark Royal* in the early months of the war. This aircraft was in use from *Resolution* during the Norwegian Campaign of April–June 1940. It was damaged by bombs off Skaanland on 16 May and towed to Harstad by a coaster, then shipped home on a merchantman for repair.

enemy destroyers and then spotting for the RN's fall of shot. They were also able to spot torpedoes in the water and warn the RN vessels. Finally, they took the opportunity to join the attack directly when the submarine *U-64* was seen at anchor off Bjerkvik. Rice dived at the submarine and released the two 100lb anti-submarine bombs, which were usually rather ineffective weapons, but on this occasion one of them may have passed through the forward hatch — in any case, the bombs proved catastrophic for *U-64* which immediately reared up into the air and began to sink, the crew swimming for their lives. For their actions that day, Rice and Brown were awarded the DSM and DSC respectively, and Admiral Whitworth considered it unlikely that a ship-borne aircraft "had ever been used to such good purpose".

The Swordfish from *Furious*' squadrons were heavily involved too, assigned to numerous tasks despite being few in number. Her aircraft were first sent out on an anti-submarine patrol ahead of *Warspite* as she sailed up Vestfjord, with patrols over Baroy Island and Ramnes at the entrance to Ofotfjord, and finally, a strike force directed against the destroyers again. The Baroy patrol reported that there were no defences on the island that could affect the operation, though the Ramnes patrol was turned away by poor weather.

Troubridge's report on the strike force reads as follows: "The Narvik force consisting of nine machines gallantly led by Captain A.R. Burch, Royal Marines with Lieutenant D. Sanderson, Royal Navy as his observer, fought their way through the Narrows into Ofotfjord with a ceiling of 500 feet and snow squalls that occasionally reduced visibility to a few yards." The ceiling lifted to 3,000 feet as the aircraft arrived on the scene, revealing the RN destroyers in action with the German ships.

> The arrival of the Fleet Air Arm at the psychological moment added a finishing touch to a situation already dramatic in the extreme and must have had a material effect on the already waning morale of the enemy. In actual fact only two direct hits were secured by heavy bombs, but the weather conditions were all against accurate bombing.[7]

The conditions were very nearly against a safe return to the carrier too, but Lieutenant Sanderson perfectly navigated the 150-mile journey, 60 miles of which were over sea, and the crews, becoming more expert now with experience, landed on "in record time" despite 50mph gusts and severe pitching. This elicited a signal from the Commander-in-Chief (CinC), "manoeuvre well executed".[8] Two Swordfish were lost to anti-aircraft fire, with two of the crew missing and one wounded (the fourth presumably recovered unharmed).

The following day, a reconnaissance flight revealed 11 enemy aircraft on a frozen lake north of Narvik, and that evening, nine Swordfish led by Lieutenant-Commander H.H. Gardner flew off to bomb and strafe them, which was successfully achieved, the crews taking such pains to leave no machine intact that the last Swordfish did not return until after dark. One aircraft, that commanded by observer Lieutenant Marshall, was hit and caught fire. The pilot, Sub-Lieutenant Ball, had the presence of mind to put the aircraft into a steep dive, which put the fire out, but after turning back over the sea, Ball found that the fuel gauge had gone from showing 90 gallons to 60 in just a few minutes, and shortly afterwards, 20 gallons. Fortunately, the Swordfish had flown over HMS *Zulu*, so was able to return and ditch alongside. Four more machines were damaged but made it back to *Furious*. One officer was wounded.

Unfortunately, the Allies lacked the land forces to follow up on the destruction of the Kriegsmarine ships, and the Heer garrison was not dislodged. By 20 April, operational losses and accidents had reduced *Furious*' air wing to nine aircraft. When the weather allowed, the carrier flew off armed reconnaissance flights to Narvik and Vestfjord on behalf of the Flag Officer, Narvik. These were carried out in challenging conditions, and one of the four Swordfish sent out was shot down, while another had to find its way back flying a few feet above the water so fierce were the snowstorms higher up. Sanderson, navigating, described it as the worst flight of his life. Weather conditions remained bad, hampering efforts to fly reconnaissance missions over the German positions. *Furious* lost one, then two of her four turbines, and as a result could do no more. She returned to the Clyde on 29 April, after three weeks away.

Furious' time on station had been frustrating in some respects, but had provided several valuable lessons. The ability of Swordfish to operate in extreme weather conditions was a useful feature in mitigating the aircraft's low performance. Remarkably, no aircraft failed to return through getting lost, an astonishing feat in such poor visibility. Although the attacks on enemy shipping had not resulted in any particular success, many lessons were learned which helped with future operations. Interestingly, the one vessel sunk by a Swordfish was the submarine destroyed by *Warspite*'s floatplane (itself shortly to be replaced by a Walrus).

Captain Troubridge summed up his feelings about *Furious*' young Swordfish crews thus:

> It is difficult to speak without emotion of the pluck and endurance of the young officers and men, some of them Midshipmen [and consequently under the age of

21], who flew their aircraft to such good effect ... All were firing their first shot whether torpedo, bomb or machine gun in action, many made their first night landing on 11 April and undeterred by the loss of several of their shipmates, their honour and courage remained throughout as dazzling as the snow covered mountains over which they so triumphantly flew.

With the withdrawal of HMS *Furious*, the arrival of *Glorious* and *Ark Royal* came not a day too soon. Operation *DX* commenced on 23 April, to provide air support to Allied ground forces, including the delivery of RAF Gloster Gladiator fighters to be operated from a temporary airfield on a frozen lake. *Ark Royal* had with her 810 and 820 Squadrons (having embarked the latter in place of 821 Squadron, which decamped to Evanton). *Glorious* was temporarily without most of her Swordfish, having disembarked 812 and 825 Squadrons, and part of 823 NAS too, to make room for the RAF Gladiators.

The immediate objective for the two carriers' Swordfish was to attack enemy aerodromes and ships in the Trondheim area. The TSRs were also required to carry out constant anti-submarine patrols, an unglamorous but essential part of aerial operations while the fleet was on station.

On Thursday, 25 April, 14 Swordfish (six from 820 and eight from 810 Squadrons) flew off *Ark Royal* to bomb Vaernes airfield and Jonsvatnet Lake, each armed with four 250lb general-purpose (GP) bombs plus eight 20lb bombs. The two carriers' Skuas were also taking part, but had orders to stay with the Swordfish after their own attacks to protect the TSRs should any enemy fighters appear. The Swordfish appear to have caught Vaernes airfield unawares, and 820 Squadron destroyed two hangars (with direct hits by Lieutenants Boulding and Hunter) plus other buildings, and 810 Squadron arriving a little later hit another hangar, buildings and a large bomber/transport aircraft. A Norwegian officer who had escaped from Trondheim later confirmed that the raid had also destroyed a fuel dump and wrecked five aircraft.

Although no Swordfish were lost through enemy action, one 810 NAS machine ditched just after take-off thanks to engine failure, and another three were lost on the way back, one from each squadron ditching safely, and an 810 Squadron machine disappearing without trace after getting separated from its sub-flight.

One of the more unusual uses for a Swordfish during this phase was to fly a message to the sloop HMS *Black Swan* to inform her that her codes had probably been compromised, and including instructions to reset her code-setting device. The aircraft arrived over *Black Swan* in the middle of a heavy bombing attack and "its task was completed under most hazardous circumstances".[9] An under-appreciated use of the Swordfish was as a photo-reconnaissance aircraft: on 27 April, an aircraft from *Ark Royal* was sent to capture oblique photographs of the forts at the entrance to Trondheim harbour, carrying out an attack on a submarine on the return journey for good measure.

A follow-up raid against Vaernes aerodrome was carried out early on 28 April with 12 Swordfish, which destroyed the last remaining hangar thanks to an accurate salvo from Lieutenant Godfrey-Paussett of 820 Squadron, and other buildings. This time, all the Swordfish returned safely, though some of them had received damage from the intense ground fire.

Vice-Admiral Wells, the officer in charge of aircraft carriers, reported: "The attacks on Vaernes aerodrome by Swordfish aircraft of Nos. 810 and 820 Squadrons were well carried out and most effective. It is remarkable that these slow aircraft twice succeeded in attacking an enemy air base without suffering a single casualty from enemy action."[10] The carriers began to withdraw to the north-west on the 28th.

An embarrassed-looking Lieutenant RN pilot is given a piggyback ashore by a long-suffering rating from Swordfish floatplane Y5G of 764 Squadron, Lee-on-Solent, the seaplane training squadron established in April 1940. Swordfish were the most common catapult aircraft for RN battleships and battle-cruisers at the outbreak of the war, but were soon replaced in that role by the Supermarine Walrus.

Useful though the Swordfish had been, it was Skuas that were in serious demand for maintaining a fighter umbrella over the embattled ground forces – three Swordfish (and a Walrus) were disembarked at Hatston to make room for more of the monoplanes when the task force returned to Norway. However, *Glorious* had now re-embarked 12 Swordfish after flying off the RAF fighters earlier in the operation. At this point, the TSRs were chiefly used for anti-submarine patrols. One such aircraft had an uncomfortable encounter on 1 May, taking hits from machine-gun fire when it was attacked by a Junkers Ju 87 Stuka that had just dive-bombed the RN warships. By this time, Namsos and Åndalsnes were being evacuated, and things were looking bleak for the Allied attempts to prevent total Axis victory in Norway. The German invasion of France in May sealed Norway's fate completely, and it soon became apparent that all forces would have to be evacuated.

At the beginning of June, *Ark Royal* went north to cover the withdrawal from Narvik and an amphibious operation to destroy the port, while *Glorious* flew off half of 823 Squadron's Swordfish so as to be able to recover RAF fighters that had been operating from frozen lakes. Swordfish from *Ark Royal* carried out reconnaissance and attacked railway targets until the 25th, while on 17 May, six aircraft of 823 Squadron flying from *Glorious* laid magnetic mines, a first for FAA aircraft, in Haugesund Channel.

During this period, 812 and 825 Squadrons, which had been detached from HMS *Glorious*, were operating under RAF Coastal Command against U-boats, E-boats and transport shipping in the Calais area during the Dunkirk evacuation. They would not see their parent carrier again. For reasons that have never been adequately explained, *Glorious* was returning from Norway with only two destroyers for escort and no Swordfish flying patrols when she was caught and sunk by the battle-cruisers *Scharnhorst* and *Gneisenau*. A desperate effort to arm and range a few of her remaining 823 Squadron Swordfish to attack the ships came to nothing when a shell destroyed the lift that was bringing an aircraft up from the hangar. The squadron effectively lost half its strength, but was able to continue operating from Hatston with nine aircraft.

There was a strong desire for a revenge attack, and *Scharnhorst* was potentially within reach; the vessel was sighted in Trondheimfjord having been damaged by one of *Glorious*' escorts. *Ark Royal*'s squadrons were detailed to carry out a raid; initially her Swordfish were to be involved along with the Skuas, but in June there was effectively no darkness that far north, and the TSRs would have been slaughtered by the Luftwaffe fighters then assembled at Vaernes. The striking force was reduced to a force of 15 Skuas, which lost more than half its strength in the attempt, doing no damage to *Scharnhorst*.

The Swordfish were to get their chance though, when *Scharnhorst* put to sea to return to Kiel after temporary repairs at Trondheim. Swordfish from 821 and 823 Squadrons flew from RNAS Hatston to the extreme edge of their combat radius in an effort to cause more harm to the battle-cruiser, but unfortunately scored no hits and lost two aircraft into the bargain. It was no doubt a risk worth taking, but the chances of success were relatively low; neither squadron had been able to carry out torpedo practice for months and many of the crews had little or no experience in torpedo attack.

It is notable that even this early in the war voices were calling for the urgent replacement of the Swordfish. During the latter stages of the Norwegian campaign, Admiral Sir Charles Forbes wrote to the Admiralty that "The skill and determination displayed by the flying crews is worthy of a better vehicle."[11] He later said: "Our FAA aircraft are hopelessly outclassed by anything that flies in the air and the sooner we get some efficient aircraft, the better." He added that the only future use he could see for Swordfish was that "if armed with cannon [they] could be used for anti E-boat operations".[12]

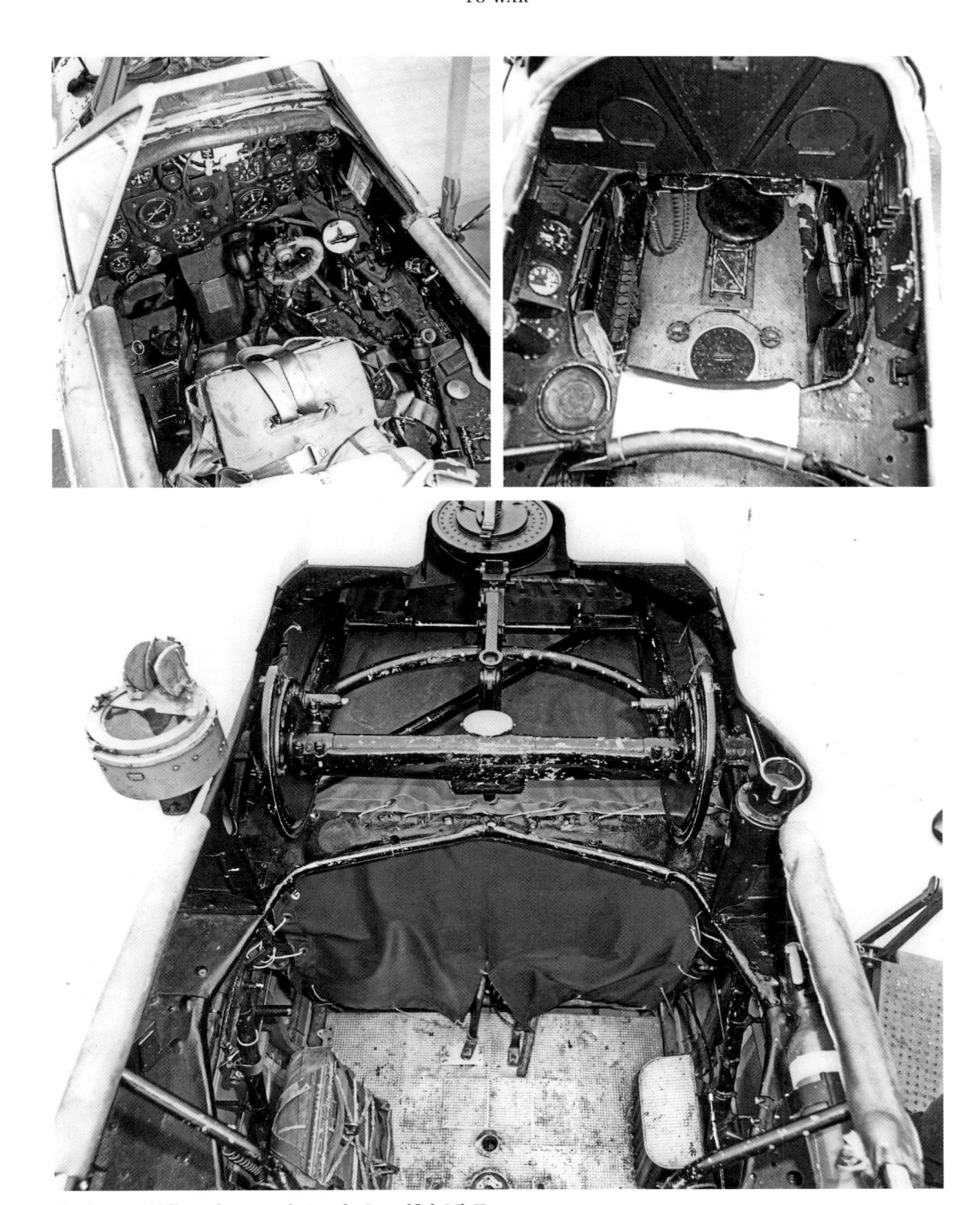

The front, middle and rear cockpits of a Swordfish Mk II.

4

THE MEDITERRANEAN

On 10 June, shortly before *Ark Royal*'s disastrous last mission in Norway, Italy declared war on Britain. This turned the Mediterranean from a safe backwater, which the FAA could use to train up new crews, into a cauldron. It also split the sea down the middle, forcing the RN to operate in two largely separate forces, the main Mediterranean Fleet based at Alexandria under Admiral Cunningham covering the eastern sector, with Somerville's Force H in the west based at Gibraltar.

As Italy entered the war, at Hyères de Palyvestre near Toulon, 767 Squadron had been quietly carrying out deck-landing training using HMS *Argus*, its instructors drawn from pilots of *Courageous*' former Swordfish squadrons. Finding itself in a theatre of war overnight, the squadron was quickly made operational. Four days after war was declared, nine Swordfish from this unit carried out the first British naval air raid on Italy, bombing Genoa with what was described as "'borrowed' and pre-fused French bombs".[13] The raid was coordinated with a squadron of Lioré et Olivier LeO 45s from the Armée de l'Air which raided Italian airfields, and can be seen as a chiefly symbolic statement of the Fleet Air Arm's willingness to contribute in the theatre. Future efforts would have more practical effects.

After the Genoa raid, 767 Squadron flew to Bône in Algeria. Here, it split into two. One part was formally made operational, being redesignated 830 Squadron on 22 June and moving to Hal Far, Malta. The remaining crews deemed to require further training, returned home with their aircraft via Casablanca and Gibraltar. Just over a week after 830 got its new 'number plate', its crews were in action conducting a night raid on the oil tanks at Augusta on Sicily. For the most part though, this unit would chiefly be involved in harrying Axis convoys from Italy to North Africa. Attacks were generally made at night so as to avoid the attentions of fighters from Sicily.

After HMS *Eagle*'s lengthy refit at Singapore, resulting from the bomb that had gone off in her handling room, she returned to the Mediterranean and was ready for operational service once again by the end of June 1940. As one of the smaller fleet carriers, she did not carry a fighter squadron, her air complement consisting of 18 Swordfish of 813 and 824 Squadrons. (The former squadron took on a 'fighter flight' of three Sea Gladiators which had belonged to HMS *Glorious* for air defence, flown by Swordfish pilots.)

While on anti-submarine patrol on 30 June, Lieutenant Young of 824 Squadron spotted an Italian submarine and dropped a stick of six

The much-patched and panel-replaced Swordfish T4W of 767 Squadron in 1940. Swordfish from this unit were the first to strike a blow for the Fleet Air Arm in the Mediterranean theatre by bombing Genoa with borrowed French bombs. The reason for 'DIB' marked on the aft fuselage in place of a serial is unknown. (MARGARET SAYER, VIA DAVID MCNAUGHT)

100lb anti-submarine bombs on the point where it submerged, but it seemed unlikely that any damage was caused, not least as only two of the bombs were observed to have gone off. The 100lb bomb was not generally successful, being too light a weapon and unreliable, and was soon supplanted by larger and more effective weapons. From October 1940, orders of the bomb were cancelled and it was often replaced in service with a simple modification of the standard Mk VII depth charge, with a detachable nose and tail for air dropping.

Eagle's squadrons would soon be in action against the Italian Navy, the Regia Marina, but before that, the FAA found itself mobilising against a recent ally. France had signed an armistice with Germany on 22 June, under the new Vichy government led by Marshal Pétain, which caused alarm in Britain. While the powerful ships of the Marine Nationale, the French Navy, were not to be handed over to Germany, their very existence posed a threat to the RN in the Mediterranean, in the event that they might be seized by the Kriegsmarine or the Vichy regime and enter the war on Germany's side.

While the French ships in Alexandria were disarmed through successful negotiation, those in Mers-el-Kébir, Oran and Dakar refused to submit to British requests to disarm or join the Allies and therefore the RN staged a series of attacks on the vessels in their ports in a series of actions under the codename Operation *Catapult*. These included

Prototype K4190 was rebuilt with dual controls in February 1937, distinguished by the second windscreen and prominent headrest fairing on the aft cockpit. The anti-spin strakes were removed, being found to be unnecessary.

strikes with bombs and torpedoes carried out by aircraft from *Ark Royal* at Mers-el-Kébir and Oran, and aircraft from *Hermes* at Dakar down the Atlantic coast of West Africa.

Ark Royal sailed to the Mediterranean after the Trondheim operation concluded, and joined Force H under Vice-Admiral James Somerville, which was constituted on 28 June. Her air group was now made up of three Swordfish squadrons – 810 with 12 aircraft and 818 and 820 each with nine aircraft.

In the evening of 3 July, Swordfish from *Ark Royal* launched a bombing attack on the heavy ships in Mers-el-Kébir and the light vessels and submarines at Oran. Vice-Admiral Wells, the senior officer in command of aircraft carriers, aboard *Ark Royal*, assessed that one hit with a 250lb bomb and one hit with a torpedo had been made on the battle-cruiser *Strasbourg* as she attempted to leave the harbour, but in reality, all the Swordfish had missed. *Ark Royal*'s Swordfish also laid mines outside the harbour entrance.

Ark Royal's Swordfish tried again three days later, with a concerted torpedo attack against the battle-cruiser *Dunkerque*, which had already been damaged by several large-calibre strikes from HMS *Hood* and her bow was resting on the bottom close to shore. The Swordfish attacked in three waves, the first wave going in at 0615, catching the crew of the battle-cruiser completely unprepared, with no defences manned. Even though *Dunkerque* was stationary and initially undefended, she was not the easiest target, being in water that was shallower than ideal for torpedoes, and partially blocked by smaller vessels. The shallow water meant the release had to be carried out as close to the water as possible, as there was not the depth for the usual dive and ascent to the correct running depth. None of the

K5996, seen being launched from the catapult at RAF Gosport, was converted into a dual control trainer in early 1939 and was subsequently occupied on catapult training from May that year to October 1942.

torpedoes hit *Dunkerque* herself, though one from the second wave hit the patrol boat *Teurre-Neuve*, moored alongside, detonating 14 depth charges; the resulting explosion caused significant damage to the battle-cruiser. Indeed, had the captain not ordered the immediate flooding of the warship's magazines when the first Swordfish was spotted, the attack could have been catastrophic. As it was, she was so badly damaged she could not be repatriated to France for repair until February 1942.[14] This represented the first major warship that Swordfish had seriously damaged. It would not be the last.

On 8 July, it was the turn of HMS *Hermes*, waiting off Dakar, and her Swordfish. A covert attempt to sink the new battleship *Richelieu* at her moorings with depth charges dropped from a small boat, failed, and the only possibility remaining was an air attack. Six aircraft of 814 NAS flew off early in the morning, attacking at dawn. Only one torpedo struck, but it did considerable damage, tearing a hole in the battleship's stern and wrecking its propulsion. She had to be towed into port, and despite efforts to prevent flooding, settled on the bottom. It's thought that the 814 Squadron torpedo may have detonated one of the depth charges sitting below the battleship from the earlier attempt, but whatever the exact cause, Swordfish had crippled two major units of a powerful navy in three days.[15] There was no little irony in the fact that the ships belonged to a very recent ally, the country from which the first Swordfish operation in the theatre had launched from.

While *Ark Royal* and *Hermes* concerned themselves with the French Navy, in the eastern and central Mediterranean, *Eagle* and her aircraft were still focused on the Italians. A convoy from Italy had reached Tobruk unmolested, but RAF reconnaissance showed a number of warships and merchantmen in the harbour. Nine Swordfish of 813 Squadron which had disembarked to Dekheila, followed up a raid by RAF Blenheims on 5 July with their own (rather more successful) dusk raid armed with torpedoes. A destroyer, the *Zeffiro*, was sunk, a second destroyer, the *Euro*, was damaged and partially flooded, while three merchant ships were sunk or severely damaged.

Swordfish had sunk and caused heavy damage to surface combatants from two navies in a matter of days. And yet, the Swordfish had not yet carried out the role envisaged for it when it was created – attacking an enemy battle fleet at sea during a fleet engagement. That omission would be rectified the day after the attack on *Richelieu*, at the Battle of Calabria, an inconclusive skirmish with the Regia Marina which nonetheless opened the Swordfish's score against the Italian Navy. The Italian fleet was at sea covering a convoy to Libya, while the Royal Navy was similarly covering two convoys between Malta and Alexandria. In the morning of 7 July, an RN destroyer spotted the two Italian battleships and reported this to

A severe accident aboard HMS *Eagle* in early 1942 resulted in two Swordfish Is of 824 Squadron wrecked. This squadron, while aboard *Eagle*, was a veteran of many successful operations in the western Mediterranean, Red Sea and South Atlantic, but ceased to exist when *Eagle* was sunk during Operation *Pedestal* in August 1942.

Vice-Admiral Cunningham, Commander-in-Chief Mediterranean Station. Cunningham immediately moved to try and cut the Italian fleet off from its base at Taranto. The Italian commander, Vice-Admiral Campioni, sought to draw the British within range of air attack to strengthen his position.

The Italian naval forces consisted of three groups — the first, comprising light forces only, was the convoy's close escort, which was supported at a distance by two groups with larger warships, one with six heavy cruisers and another with two battleships and eight light cruisers, as well as destroyers. The RN force was similarly split into three groups, a cruiser squadron, the battleship *Warspite* with escorting destroyers, and the battleships *Malaya* and *Royal Sovereign* with escorting destroyers, the last of which *Eagle* was sailing with.

Even with the necessary preparations for a strike mission to be made, *Eagle*'s Swordfish had to maintain the usual anti-submarine patrol. On the 7th, these spotted two submarines and one was attacked with bombs, but without clear results. With the enemy at sea, the work only increased, with three aircraft flown off at 0440 on 9 July to try to pinpoint Campioni's heavy ships, and a further three flown off at 0858, to search a narrower quadrant as far distant as they could manage. At 1026 the first sighting was reported, with *Eagle*'s 'B' and 'C' search aircraft each making a separate sighting, and 'D' noting two battleships and five cruisers at 1105.

Unfortunately, the presence of a single carrier only, and a small one at that, compromised the operation. *Eagle* was preparing to launch relief shadowers to keep the enemy battle fleet under observation, but received the order to launch an immediate strike before this could be done. Before the strike force reached the Italian fleet, it made a turn to the south and as the British force lacked a shadower on station, the Swordfish had no way of knowing this. This, together with the difficulty of distinguishing battleships and cruisers from the air, caused considerable confusion over which group of warships was which. The 813 NAS striking force did, however, locate a group of enemy ships at 1230 and spent the next hour working round into position, diving in at 1330 and concentrating on the two ships at the rear of the line. No hits were observed and as the ships were travelling fast and manoeuvring vigorously, it appears none was made.

However, the main Italian fleet was located again before long, by relief aircraft 'C' at 1440, and another striking force (this time from 824 Squadron) was flown off at 1539, by which time the two opposing fleets were in contact at very long range. The leader, Lieutenant-Commander A.J. Debenham, went in to attack what he thought was a battleship but realised while in the attack that it was probably a Bolzano-class cruiser. All aircraft attacked the same target, and Debenham said of the second sub-flight in particular that "This attack was very well executed and pressed well home." There was relatively little anti-aircraft fire, which was a great relief to the crews. Several crews reported either smoke or a water columns from suspected hits, and the dropping positions were good but only one 'probable' hit was claimed, and even this was optimistic.

Twenty minutes after the second strike was flown off, another Swordfish was launched to act as a spotter for *Royal Sovereign*. Meanwhile, *Warspite*'s Swordfish floatplane was carrying out the same function, as it had at Narvik, and this may have contributed to the hit the battleship scored on *Guilio Cesare* at 1559, the longest-range hit by a naval gun at sea in history.

When the second strike force returned at 1705, maintainers launched into feverish activity to try and prepare as many aircraft as possible for a third strike. By this time there were no 'ready use' torpedoes available and more had to be brought up from the storage room. Six aircraft of 813 Squadron had been readied by 1750, when a general recall of aircraft ordered by the commander-in-chief abruptly ended *Eagle*'s efforts.

The lack of results was frustrating, and hid what had been a near-miraculous performance from *Eagle*'s aircrews and maintainers. Two squadrons of Swordfish had been operated constantly for a nine-hour period. Being the only carrier present, *Eagle*'s aircraft had to juggle all of the anti-submarine patrol duties, reconnaissance and shadowing, as well as muster a strike force. Moreover, with no Skuas, the Swordfish had to carry out the aerial attacks alone, without the FAA's preferred combined dive-bombing and torpedo strike to divide a target's attention and defences.

Nevertheless, there were many positives to take from the experience. Cunningham wrote: "The torpedo attacks by the Fleet Air Arm were disappointing, one hit on a cruiser being all that can be claimed, but in fairness it must be recorded that the pilots had had very little practice, and none at high speed targets, *Eagle* having only recently joined the Fleet."

He added:

I cannot conclude these remarks without a reference to HMS *Eagle*. This obsolescent aircraft carrier, with only 17 Swordfish embarked, found and kept touch with the enemy fleet, flew off two striking forces of 9 torpedo bombers within the space of 4 hours, both of which attacked, and all aircraft returned. 24 hours later a torpedo striking force was launched on shipping in Augusta and throughout the 5 days operations *Eagle* maintained constant A/S [anti-submarine] patrols in daylight and carried out several searches. Much of *Eagle*'s aircraft operating work was done in the fleeting intervals between, and even during, bombing attacks and I consider her performance reflects great credit on Captain A.M. Bridge, Royal Navy, her Commanding Officer.[16]

The Swordfish of 824 and 813 Squadrons were not finished yet, however. The day after the main action at sea, the RN forces reassembled to escort the slow convoy MS1, but an RAF flying boat reported a number of heavy units of the Regia Marina in port at Augusta, Sicily. Indeed, much of the fleet had repaired there to refuel after the action off Calabria, and this was felt to be too good an opportunity for *Eagle*'s aircraft to miss. A striking force of nine 813 NAS Swordfish was flown off at 1850, and crossed the Malta Channel led by Lieutenant-Commander Kennedy in three sub-flights, approaching the coast at 'zero feet'. The squadron split up at 2115.

Unfortunately for 813 Squadron, all but a few ships had left Augusta by this time. Radio intercepts had warned them that a raid was coming, and the majority of the fleet had dispersed. All Kennedy and the two aircraft with him could see as they flew over the harbour, having not yet attracted the attention of Italian defences, were two ships which they identified as a destroyer and an oiler. The destroyer was the large, Navigatori-class destroyer *Leone Pancaldo*, which had finished refuelling a little earlier and was moored in the middle of the harbour, ready to depart. Kennedy made for *Pancaldo* and launched his torpedo at 400 yards, seeing a large column of water just as he turned away. He reported "the destroyer seemed to have broken in two and was undoubtedly sinking". Kennedy noted that the next aircraft, flown by Lieutenant Keith, aimed at the other vessel but saw his torpedo turn away to starboard and miss. Lieutenant Collins, following behind, saw no further targets and launched at the *Pancaldo*.

Italian sources suggest that in fact, Kennedy's torpedo missed *Pancaldo* altogether, exploding against a cliff, and it was Collins' 'fish' that hit and sank the destroyer. The ship that Keith, meanwhile, had actually been aiming at was a second destroyer, *Ugolino Vivaldi*. It was tied up by the refuelling mole and this with the poor visibility made it difficult to make out her silhouette.[17]

Lieutenant Drummond spotted two submarines on the way into the harbour, and went back to look for them after initially finding no suitable targets within. There were no longer any submarines to be seen, so Drummond went back over the harbour a second time, launching at the 'oiler' from its starboard quarter. The observer, Midshipman Todd, thought he saw a column of water where the target should be, but the torpedo ran aground in shallow water and failed to detonate. All the other aircraft, finding no suitable targets, returned to *Eagle* with their torpedoes. The *Pancaldo* had not broken in two as Kennedy thought, but could not be kept afloat and sank in the harbour. The hull was found to be relatively sound, and she was eventually refloated and returned to service, though she was out of the war for a full two years.

The raid had not reaped anything like the results that *Eagle*'s fliers had hoped for, but it did prove that a night raid against an enemy in port was viable, and provided a number of lessons about how to make the most of it. This would prove highly important just a few months later.

However, the poor overall performance of the Swordfish (along with other types) was the cause of increasing concern in naval circles. Sir Charles Forbes, Commander-in-Chief of the Home Fleet, wrote to the Admiralty on 18 July noting among the officers and men of the FAA, "A feeling of exasperation that their efforts should be so handicapped by the necessity of operating aircraft of such relatively low performance," adding, "there is no getting away from the fact that the Walrus, the Swordfish and the Skua ... are the slowest aircraft of their respective types in the world."

Nevertheless, the Swordfish were getting results, even if this was overshadowed by disappointment that they had not, mostly through bad luck and poor intelligence, achieved even more. After Calabria, *Eagle* put back into Alexandria and her aircraft disembarked, 813 Squadron to M'aten Bagush, and 824 Squadron to Sidi Barrani. On 20 July the latter was sent on a repeat of the earlier mission to Tobruk where enemy warships were known to be in the harbour. This time the raid was carried out at night, by moonlight, without any diversion by the RAF. Despite the same kind of visibility and target identification issues that affected the attack on Augusta, the squadron sank two destroyers, the *Nembo* and *Ostro*, and a merchant ship, the *Sereno*.

Meanwhile, 813 Squadron had been detached under RAF control in order to respond quickly to reconnaissance reports. Just such a report on the morning of 22 August revealed a destroyer, several submarines and a depot ship in port at Ain el Gazala on the Gulf of Bomba, so three aircraft, led by Captain 'Ollie' Patch (a Royal Marine) took off at 1000 armed with torpedoes. Yet again, the Swordfish seemed to catch the Regia Marina in port unawares, and Patch was able to release his torpedo at a submarine at point-blank range virtually unopposed. "Within a few seconds we saw a huge explosion amidships on the submarine which split in two, the bows quickly disappearing while the stern stuck up in the air,"[18] recounted Lieutenant Wellham in the second aircraft. He swung to starboard, while Lieutenant Cheesman in the third Swordfish went to port, both aircraft closing on the depot ship from opposite sides. As the Swordfish approached, they saw a destroyer and another submarine tied up beside the depot ship, and both launched their torpedoes at this tempting target, seeing "a tremendous explosion and a vast cloud of black smoke tinged with flame [shooting] hundreds of feet into the air".[19]

This raid was much celebrated as the "attack which achieved the phenomenal result of the destruction of four enemy ships with three torpedoes", as Cunningham's dispatch to the Admiralty put it. According to most British reports, aerial reconnaissance the next day revealed that both submarines and both surface vessels had been sunk, and also that Italian radio confirmed this. However, subsequent Italian admissions of losses were restricted to the submarine *Iride* and

The end met by numerous Swordfish on carriers at sea: too badly damaged to repair on the ship and too inconvenient to take up space in the hangar, they were stripped of all useful parts (in this photo it can be seen that the removable panels on the aft fuselage are missing).

auxiliary minelayer *Monte Gargano*. Whichever was correct, it was another feather in the cap of *Eagle*'s squadrons, and reinforced the notion that attacks on enemy ships in port could reap considerable rewards. The real benefit, unknown at that time, was that the *Iride* was no ordinary submarine. She had been modified for carriage of three '*maiale*' ('pig') human torpedoes, and having trialled these successfully, had put in to Ain el Gazala in order to carry out an imminent attack on the Mediterranean Fleet in Alexandria. It would be over a year before the Regia Marina was finally able to realise this ambition; 813 NAS had unknowingly prevented a significant shift in the balance of naval power in the Mediterranean.

Furthermore, the fact that Swordfish could operate reliably in relatively harsh and primitive conditions, and its aircrews navigate long distances over open water with no modern aids also augured well for this technically obsolete aircraft playing an important part in the war to come.

The determination of the Swordfish aircrews was another factor in their favour. Navigation on the Gulf of Bomba raid was done by Midshipman Woodley, who carried out his task "with great accuracy" and "coolness of head", according to Captain Bridge. He insisted on taking part in the raid despite suffering from tonsillitis, and had to go immediately into sick quarters on returning. Wellham was slightly wounded in the attack, being grazed by a bullet on the ankle, but managed to fly back without difficulty.

Meanwhile, *Ark Royal*, after taking part in the

efforts to disarm the French fleet detailed above, was soon engaged against a more conventional enemy along with the rest of Force H in the western Mediterranean. On 27 July she sailed from Gibraltar for the combined operations *Hurry* and *Crush*. The former was a mission to fly off Hawker Hurricanes from HMS *Argus* for the defence of Malta, while the latter was a raid on Cagliari harbour, Sardinia, as a diversion from *Hurry*. On 2 August, at 0225, in a position roughly 125 miles west-south-west of the target, *Ark Royal* flew off 12 Swordfish, armed with a mix of bombs, mines and incendiaries. Unfortunately, one aircraft collided with the carrier's island and crashed over the side. Lieutenant Robins, Lieutenant J. Tarver and Petty Officer Clarke of 810 NAS were all killed. The rest formed up over flame floats, which had been positioned some five miles away from the fleet, and flew on to Cagliari.

The intention had been to attack at dawn, but changes in the wind and difficulty finding the target meant that when the Swordfish finally reached the port, it was in full daylight. As a result, the Swordfish flew into a storm of anti-aircraft fire as they approached the targets — Elmas airfield and the harbour. Nevertheless, according to Captain Holland, commanding *Ark Royal*, "The bombing attacks appeared to be very successful, direct hits on hangars being obtained, aerodrome buildings and hangars set on fire, two large aircraft on sea wall and two aeroplanes at moorings being destroyed and others damaged."[20]

Mines were laid in the entrance to the outer harbour. Aircraft 4F (P4127) was noticed losing height and jettisoning its bombs during the attack on the airfield, and indeed, this machine had been hit by anti-aircraft fire. The pilot, Lieutenant Humphries, made a successful forced-landing on the runway and he and his two crewmembers were taken prisoner. The aircraft was relatively little damaged and was later repaired and re-engined with an Alfa Romeo radial and was assessed at the Guidonia Flight Test Centre. All other aircraft made it back to *Ark Royal*, though some were damaged. One of the crew, Sub-Lieutenant Watt, was slightly wounded.

It was during this operation that one of the only known instances of a Swordfish acting as an interceptor took place. Aircraft A2M on fleet reconnaissance made "several determined attacks" on a CANT Z.506 seaplane off Cape Spartivento, and "due to skilful manoeuvring, several attacks were pressed home by this slow aircraft on the enemy before the latter realised the situation and opening his throttle, made off".[21]

The following month, however, *Ark Royal* would be back in the Atlantic facing French forces in Operation *Menace*, a strange mix of gunboat diplomacy and amphibious warfare. Operation *Menace* was an attempt to boost the embryonic Free French cause of Charles de Gaulle by persuading French Senegal to switch to the Allies, or failing that, seize the port of Dakar by force. The carrier's Swordfish were initially employed on 'D-Day' dropping leaflets over the town, and in the case of one aircraft, escorting two small aircraft carrying members of a delegation to negotiate with the Vichy authorities. This aircraft, while it was observing the landing of the negotiators' aircraft, noticed Curtiss Hawk 75 fighters being scrambled, and radioed this back to the carrier. By then, the Swordfish was under AA fire, and beat a hasty retreat, and all Swordfish apart from the anti-submarine patrols were also recalled. The A/S patrol spotted two submarines, *Ajax* and *Persée*, leaving the harbour, and later one of the patrolling aircraft carried out an attack on the former, without success.

The following day, *Ark Royal*'s aircraft were launched to attack the forces firing on the Allied warships, with Skuas dive-bombing the battleship *Richelieu* and six Swordfish of 820 NAS bombing Fort Manoel, and its 240mm guns. Several hits were claimed but little damage seems to have been done and the battery continued firing unabated. Later that morning, nine 810 Squadron Swordfish

Two shots of Swordfish in repair shops. The economies of repairing even badly damaged aircraft were firmly established for British air arms in 1940, and as a result, extensive facilities were established to repair aircraft. The nature of the Swordfish, with a bolted-up spaceframe fuselage structure and numerous removable and replaceable panels, made it eminently repairable even when large parts of the airframe were wrecked.

flew off armed with torpedoes to attack *Richelieu*, but this time they scored no hits and three of the aircraft were shot down. Another three aircraft were lost throughout the day, most of the crews becoming prisoners of war, though one aircraft ditched near a British ship and the crew was recovered. The submarine *Bévéziers* snuck out of the harbour and reported on the movements of the British ships, also attempting to line up for an attack. She was several times spotted and attacked by Swordfish from the A/S patrol and although no damage was inflicted on the submarine, the attacks prevented her from attaining a firing solution, and at 1700 her captain gave up and returned to port to recharge batteries.

Operation *Menace* was an unmitigated failure, and *Ark Royal*'s Swordfish squadrons suffered significant losses for no reward. They were not quite finished, as the submarine *Sidi-Ferruch* had pursued the Allied ships away from Dakar and was attempting to attack *Ark Royal* when a Swordfish from the A/S patrol forced her to submerge and abandon the attempt.

After this debacle, *Ark Royal* headed to Liverpool for a refit, and would not return to the Mediterranean until early November.

Meanwhile on Malta, 830 Squadron was getting into its stride. Initially, the various authorities on Malta, at sea and back in the UK struggled, to agree on what to do with this hurriedly formed unit. At first, it was considered that they could be used as night bombers against targets on Sicily, but otherwise be available to be called upon by Cunningham. Cunningham himself preferred that they be used for anti-submarine patrol and as a torpedo strike force against surface vessels. As there were already three Swordfish on Malta from 3 Anti-Aircraft Co-operation Unit employed on anti-submarine patrol, Malta HQ was happy that 830 Squadron be used for anti-shipping strikes but also wanted them to be able to bomb targets on Sicily. In the end, this was broadly what 830 Squadron did. (Later, the three AACU aircraft were passed to 830 Squadron.)

Their first raid on Augusta's oil tanks was carried out on 30 June, and many similar raids on targets in Sicily and Libya followed. It was to be in the anti-shipping role, however, that 830 Squadron became best known.

In the summer of 1940, in fact, the only offensive missions from Malta were those carried out by 830 Squadron. There was a raid on Catania airfield, resulting in two hangars destroyed, and a raid on the harbour at Augusta with uncertain results, the second in August. Twice the squadron was scrambled to attack enemy shipping, but on each occasion failed to find the reported vessels.

*

At the end of August, the first of a new class of carriers arrived in the Mediterranean. This was HMS *Illustrious*, the first of the armoured carriers, dreamed up with the 'narrow seas' firmly in mind. Her Swordfish squadrons were 815 and 819 NAS. Finally, HMS *Eagle* and her squadrons would no longer have to carry air operations with the Mediterranean Fleet alone. *Illustrious*' first task would be to contribute to Operation *MB3*. This was itself part of Operation *Hats*, a combined operation with Force H to deliver supplies to Malta and strengthen the Mediterranean Fleet itself (of which the arrival of *Illustrious* and various other ships, including two anti-aircraft cruisers, was part).

Hopes of another fleet action were raised when one of *Eagle*'s Swordfish spotted a force of two Italian battleships and several cruisers less than 200 miles away, but were dashed when that force turned for Taranto. Cunningham, with his newly reinforced fleet, was disinclined to return to port immediately, and took the opportunity to attack airfields on Rhodes. *Illustrious*' Swordfish were detailed to attack the airfield at Kalathos (Calato). Nine aircraft of 819 Squadron and three from 815 NAS were to fly off from 0345 on 4 September, armed with a mix of high-explosive and incendiary bombs. Unfortunately, the ninth aircraft collided with the carrier's island on take-off and blocked

A Swordfish being batted onto an Illustrious-class carrier. HMS *Illustrious*, the first of the armoured carriers, was commissioned in April 1940, and in June took aboard her Swordfish squadrons, 815 and 819 NAS, joining the Mediterranean Fleet in September 1940.

the deck, preventing the last three aircraft, which included the officer detailed to lead the strike. The next most senior member of 819 NAS took over and the aircraft in the air proceeded to the target, dive-bombing buildings and parked aircraft, all aircraft completing their attack in an estimated 45 seconds. Once again, the aircraft had achieved total surprise and it was believed they had caused significant damage. There were no casualties apart from the aircraft that had crashed on take-off, and it was a good opening of the *Illustrious* squadrons' account.

Eagle, meanwhile, was experiencing difficulty with a light and variable wind, which delayed the launch of 813 and 824 NAS aircraft to attack Maritsa airfield. This may have led to the force arriving with less surprise than it might have done, especially as the Swordfish had to approach the target closer to the coast to make up time, and of course with more of the approach in daylight. Even so, the aircraft were above the airfield before the first fighters were seen taking off. Sub-Lieutenant Stovin-Bradford in the last aircraft noted hits and near-misses on hangars and other buildings, with large fires well underway as the aircraft left.

The fighters, identified as Fiat CR42 biplanes, did not manage to intercept the Swordfish before they had dropped their bombs, but several managed to attack afterwards. Four Swordfish, all belonging to 813 Squadron, failed to return and it was assumed they had been shot down.

The following month, *Illustrious*' squadrons carried out another raid (Operation *MB6*, 13/14 October), this time on Portolago on the island of Leros in the Dodecanese. Their instructions were to attack any ships they found in the harbour or, in the absence of ships, to attack port facilities including a floating dock. Workshops and seaplane hangars were left ablaze, and one aircraft attacked what was thought to be three destroyers at anchor off Brachos Point, but if there were any ships there it seems unlikely any damage was caused. Ten days later, *Illustrious* and *Eagle* combined forces for another attack on Tobruk, the main purpose of which was to lay mines in the harbour, but a few aircraft were armed with bombs to create a diversion. This subterfuge largely worked, even with the need to drop flares over the harbour to help ensure the mines were accurately placed, and most of the AA fire in the harbour was directed at the bombing aircraft. All the aircraft returned safely to Dekheila apart from L4Q, which missed a landmark and had to force-land on the Alexandria–Mersa Matruh road. On 27 October, Swordfish from *Eagle* made a dive-bombing attack on the port at Analipsi (Maltezana) on the island of Astypalaia. The Swordfish crews in the eastern Mediterranean were gaining skill and experience in making night-time attacks on ports that would soon lead to the Swordfish's greatest moment.

5

TRIUMPH AND TRAGEDY

THE FLEET Air Arm's stunning attack on the Italian battle fleet in port at Taranto has been extensively covered elsewhere so it is not the intention here to recount it in detail. However, as possibly the crowning glory of the Swordfish's career. it is important to place it in context. It represented the culmination of a series of operations that increasingly demonstrated the aircraft's utility at night. It represented the apogee of the Royal Navy's intelligent use of its asset's strengths while mitigating its shortcomings. It proved that used appropriately and flexibly, even an obsolescent carrier-launched torpedo bomber could fulfil the role foreseen for it a decade earlier.

The attack on the battle fleet was, however, just one part of a wider series of activities across the Mediterranean – Operation *MB8*. This incorporated a series of convoys, bringing supplies and defences to Malta and Greece, and shepherding empty merchant ships from Malta to Alexandria. There was also a diversionary raid on Cagliari to disrupt the bomber squadrons based at the airfield, carried out by *Ark Royal*'s aircraft on 9 November 1940, consisting of nine aircraft from 810, 818 and 820 Squadrons in the early morning. Hangars, a power station and seaplanes were destroyed for no loss, despite heavy (if not particularly accurate) AA fire.

The Italian fleet anchorage at Taranto was a constant threat to the Royal Navy in the Mediterranean, in particular the supply line to Malta. According to a study in the *Naval War College Review*, "Taranto's location was a key element of its value to the Italian navy – it was conveniently close to the British Malta-to-Suez run yet sequestered enough to be easily guarded by land-based planes." [22]

There were two factors in early November 1940 that made the success at Taranto possible that had not been present before. The first of these was long-range fuel tanks, which were first available when *Illustrious* arrived in September. These would enable the raid to be flown off from a distance where the carrier would be unlikely to be detected by enemy reconnaissance. The second was reconnaissance photographs obtained by Martin Maryland light bombers, recently obtained from the US diverted from a French order, several of which were now based at Malta. The Maryland (still generally referred to as a 'Glenn Martin' at the time) was faster and more manoeuvrable than the flying boats the RAF relied on previously for long-range photographic reconnaissance. This quite simply meant it could take photographs of targets well defended by AA guns and even fighters, where it had not previously been possible. The

Marylands gathered a series of detailed photographs of the harbour, showing the locations of the various ships at anchor and defences such as booms and nets. This intelligence was essential to a successful attack and contrasted sharply with what had been available in Norway and earlier in the Mediterranean.

These two factors suddenly being available meant that an idea that had been germinating since "long before the outbreak of war", as Cunningham pointed out in his report to the Admiralty,[23] was now practicable. According to John Wellham, one of the pilots who would take part, a plan had been devised by HMS *Glorious*' captain Lumley Lyster when Italy invaded Ethiopia in 1935, and updated during the Munich Crisis in 1938.[24] It would become reality as Operation *Judgement*.

The raid had originally been planned for 21 October, to coincide with Trafalgar Day. However, a fire in *Illustrious*' hangar destroyed several aircraft and damaged others. By the time the damage had been put right, the conditions were unsuitable. The delay did, however, allow more practice in use of flares to illuminate the target, which was judged necessary even though there would be a three-quarters-full moon.

More seriously, the mission had been to include both carriers in the eastern Mediterranean, but *Eagle* had been suffering from faults caused by various near-misses by bombs over the previous few months. Her aviation fuel lines had been fractured and repaired once too many times and the whole system was determined to be in urgent need of proper renewal in a dockyard. Rather than delay the operation again, eight of *Eagle*'s most experienced night-flying crews transferred temporarily to *Illustrious*, "so that *Eagle*, whose squadrons had reached a high state of efficiency, was to some extent represented in the attack".[25]

Before the date of the operation, another three aircraft were lost over three days, having to ditch thanks to contaminated fuel. These various setbacks reduced the striking force from 30 in the original plan to twenty-one. They would fly off in two waves, of 12 and nine aircraft respectively, each with a mix of aircraft armed with torpedoes, bombs and flares. The first aircraft took off between 2035 and 2040 on 11 November, the second wave following from 2128–2134. The aircraft flown by Lieutenant Clifford, 5F, sustained slight damage to the wing while being handled on deck, and had to be struck down for repairs. Clifford and his observer Lieutenant Going were so determined to take part they insisted on flying off alone. They took off some 24 minutes after the last aircraft of the second wave had departed.

When the first wave reached Taranto at 2256, the two illumination aircraft released a row of flares along the harbour's eastern flank, which it was hoped would silhouette the warships at anchor for the aircraft attacking from the west; the six battleships were arranged roughly in a north–south line near the eastern edge of the outer harbour. The first attack was made by Lieutenant-Commander Williamson (815 NAS) and two other aircraft that came in over San Pietro Island near the entrance to the outer harbour. Their planned target was the *Vittorio Veneto*, but Williamson was shot down over the harbour and the other two had trouble identifying the intended battleship, instead attacking the *Conte di Cavour*.

Lieutenant Kemp's aircraft aimed at the *Littorio*, towards the northern end of the line, and met fierce anti-aircraft fire from cruisers and merchant ships, which Kemp avoided by hugging the surface and dodging between the merchantmen. Lieutenant Swayne also aimed at the *Littorio*, closing to 400 yards before dropping and actually flying right over the ship to make his escape. Lieutenant Maund, aiming at the same ship, also experienced heavy AA fire from the cruisers, but flew low enough that most of it passed overhead. The other aircraft dive-bombed cruisers and destroyers in the inner harbour.

The second wave formed up and turned for

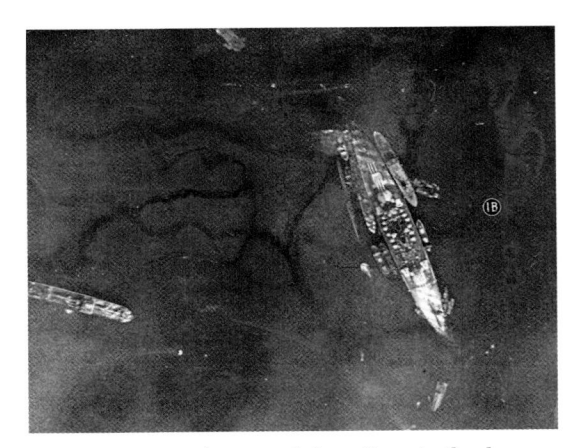

Reconnaissance photograph from Taranto the day after the raid by Swordfish from HMS *Illustrious*, showing the battleship *Littorio* with her bows (top) awash, leaking fuel oil and surrounded by tugs and support vessels.

Taranto at 2145. One of the flare-dropping aircraft lost its external long-range fuel tank and had to return to *Illustrious*, but the remaining eight continued, arriving at 2255. Once again, the flare-dropping aircraft were detached on reaching the harbour, and the rest went in to attack. Lieutenant-Commander Hale, leading the second wave, also went for the *Littorio*, as did Lieutenant Torrens-Spence, while Lieutenant Lea dropped at what he thought was the *Guilio Cesare* but was probably the *Duilio*. Wellham received a hit to his Swordfish while in the dive towards the target and was struggling for control, managing to opportunistically aim at what he identified as one of the Littorio-class battleships from the port quarter. Other aircraft bombed the oil storage depot and smaller warships. Lieutenant Bayly was shot down by AA from the cruiser *Gorizia*, and his aircraft was seen to explode.

The attack caused devastation in the Italian battle fleet. *Littorio*, one of two brand-new fast battleships, was hit by three torpedoes and holed on both sides, twice in the stern and once in the bow. She was only saved by being beached, though her bows were completely submerged. *Duilio*, a modernised First World War battleship, was hit once with a torpedo that blew a large hole in her bow, and also had to be beached to prevent her sinking. *Conte di Cavour*, another modernised First World War battleship, had an even larger hole, and sank before she could be beached, only part of her main armament and superstructure remaining above water.

Littorio, as the most valuable of the sunk battleships was the focus of a concerted effort to restore to service, but was still out of action for four months. *Duilio* was not back in service until the middle of May 1941, while *Conte di Cavour* was not even raised until June 1941, and the damage was so severe she was still not finished when Italy surrendered in September 1943. Little damage was done to cruisers and destroyers – frustratingly, bombs that hit the heavy cruiser *Trento* and several smaller vessels failed to explode – but fires were set in the dockyard and seaplane base.

The conventional view of the attack at the time was that it had been a decisive blow against the Regia Marina that permanently altered the balance of naval power in the theatre. More recent assessments have concluded that while a tactical success, the strike on Taranto had little long-term impact and represented a wasted opportunity to virtually knock the Italian Navy out of the war. Lieutenant-Colonel Angelo N. Caravaggio, Canadian Forces, for example argued that Operation *Judgement* was too important to be rolled into the wider Operation *MB8*, which weakened its impact, and suggested that the decisions on targeting and armament were poor, leaving the brand-new state-of-the-art *Vittorio Veneto* untouched.[26]

It is true that the attack did not eliminate the Regia Marina battle fleet from the equation, and Italian battleships continued to bear an influence – indeed, later that month, the presence of two of the remaining battleships at sea contributed to the partial failure of Operation *White*, an attempt to supply Malta with Hurricane fighters. Nevertheless, Taranto cast a long shadow.

It robbed the Regia Marina of one battleship for the rest of the war, and two more for many months, while diverting resources to repairs that could otherwise have advanced the building of new ships like the third and fourth Littorio-class vessels. It made the Regia Marina somewhat more conservative about committing its heavy ships, and consequently some opportunities to interfere with Allied convoys and other operations were not taken. The Italian losses at Taranto, when taken with the failure of their own raid on Alexandria, prevented a significant swing to the Axis, and gave the Allies breathing space.

It is possible that arming more aircraft with torpedoes rather than bombs would have increased the success against the battleships, but in reality, the proportion of hits was extremely high, even allowing for the stationary targets.

Crucially, the duplex pistols in the torpedoes worked remarkably reliably in view of later experience with the device. It can be regarded as a good strike rate to score five hits from 9–11 drops in view of the likelihood of torpedoes grounding in shallow water or exploding prematurely. The question of targeting is moot, as the Swordfish pilots tended to end up gravitating towards the most exposed ships. The three battleships damaged were the ones anchored in the outermost stations, and to press home and attack those anchored behind them would have meant flying uncomfortably close to at least one other battleship, while the chances of the torpedo striking the harbour bottom were significantly increased. (Indeed, several unexploded torpedoes were found afterwards in the mud.) Finally, and by no means least important, Operation *Judgement* contributed greatly to the success of Operation *MB8*, as the convoys to Malta (Operation *Coat*), Alexandria (*MW3* and *ME3*), and Piraeus (*AN6*) all got through completely unmolested.

While it is often stated that Taranto led to the Italian Fleet being confined to port for much of the rest of the war, this is an exaggeration. Indeed, the Royal Navy still regarded the Regia Marina battle fleet as a significant threat, which led to Operation *White* being severely compromised when the fighters were launched further from their destination than planned. Although the launching point was still theoretically well within the endurance of the aircraft involved, mistakes and miscalculations led to more than half the force of desperately needed Hurricanes running out of fuel. This failure can be directly attributed to the threat still posed by the remaining battleships.

Nevertheless, the removal of three battleships from the immediate equation boosted British confidence; a convoy to pass all the way through the Mediterranean to Alexandria – Operation *Collar* – was dispatched from Britain the day after the raid, reaching Gibraltar on the 24th. Italian intelligence discovered the convoy, and Admiral Campioni, with two of the three undamaged battleships, moved to intercept on 27 November. Force H, providing the heavy escort, engaged, leading to the Battle of Cape Spartivento.*

Both Somerville and Campioni handled their forces with a degree of caution (which would later lead to their fighting spirit being questioned by their respective governments). Somerville was conscious that the battleground was well within the range of land-based aircraft, and felt that chasing the Italians would pose an unacceptable risk to his force. He was also hampered, as Cunningham had been at Calabria, by the low speed of his own battleships. Campioni, on the other hand, had to contend with highly restricted rules of engagement, preventing him from engaging unless he had a high chance of success. (Indeed, he was in radio contact with Rome attempting to secure agreement to join battle even as the first shots were being fired.) He was also aware that the presence of an aircraft carrier (*Ark Royal*) and

---

* Known in Italy as the Battle of Cape Teleuda (*Battaglia di Capo Teulada*).

Swordfish Mk I L7678 '5G' of 821/X Squadron in late 1940/early 1941. This squadron had been operating as a shore-based unit from RNAS Hatston for much of 1940, and carried out an unsuccessful attack on *Scharnhorst* at extreme range in June 1940. This aircraft was one of six that formed 821X Flight when the main unit disbanded in December 1940, sailing to Malta to reinforce 830 Squadron.

her Swordfish could dramatically alter the balance of forces.

It was one of these aircraft that spotted the main Italian force, and at 1130, 11 Swordfish from 810 Squadron flew off in response. Around 45 minutes later, they spotted two battleships, *Vittorio Veneto* and *Guilio Cesare*, with their screen of destroyers and positioned to approach out of the sun. Remarkably, the lead Swordfish got within 1,500 feet of the battleships before coming under any AA fire from them, and all aircraft launched within 700 to 800 yards, inside the destroyer screen. While a hit was claimed against each battleship, Italian sources indicate that none was scored. On the opposite scale, the Italians claimed two Swordfish shot down, while in fact all returned safely to *Ark Royal*. This was the last involvement of the aircraft in the battle, which ended inconclusively when both sides withdrew after just under an hour. As a result of missing the opportunity to damage the British force, Campioni was removed from his post, while Somerville was subjected to a board of inquiry, though he was cleared by it and continued in charge of Force H.

At the beginning of December 1940, 821 Squadron (earlier part of *Ark Royal*'s air group which had been disembarked during the Norwegian campaign) disbanded, spawning 821X Flight, which was dispatched to supplement 830 Squadron on Malta. The six aircraft were transported on HMS *Argus* and received aboard *Ark Royal* on 30 December for transfer to Malta, but were in such poor condition that her captain was moved to complain to Somerville.[27] None was fitted with the necessary long-range fuel tanks, their torpedo equipment was deficient, their compasses had not been corrected, and their guns were rusty having not been cleaned since they had last been used. *Ark Royal*'s maintainers were compelled to make the aircraft good themselves, using the ship's own stock of spares. Even then, one of the aircraft went unserviceable when they were being flown off, so only five Swordfish made the flight to Hal Far on 8 January.

Two days later, HMS *Illustrious* suffered a dramatic setback, in part a response to the victory at Taranto. The specialist Luftwaffe anti-shipping unit Fliegerkorps X was transferred to the Mediterranean from Norway to assist the transfer of supplies and reinforcements to the Afrika Korps, which the carrier was clearly a threat to. On 10 January, therefore, the unit threw everything it had into knocking *Illustrious* out. After a largely diversionary attack by a few Italian torpedo bombers at 1220, which drew the covering fighters away and caused them to use up their ammunition, a large group of dive-bombers was detected. This was a threat that had not been faced before in the Mediterranean, and proved devastating. A further four attacks were made on the carrier that day. She limped into Malta, living to fight another day but only after a lengthy spell in a dockyard. It was grim proof of the benefits of building the carrier with so much protection — had she not had the armoured 'box', *Illustrious* would undoubtedly have been sunk, but many of the carrier's aircrew had been killed, and aircraft destroyed due to a fire in the hangar caused by splinters. The surviving crews of 815 and 819 Squadrons took the remaining aircraft to Hal Far. On 14 January the ex-*Illustrious* squadrons combined with 821X Flight under 815 Squadron's 'number plate', at Dekheila.

6

MALTA, THE RED SEA AND CRETE

In the western Mediterranean, *Ark Royal* continued to operate as part of Force H, using her Swordfish to take the fight to Italian forces after the setback in eastern waters. At the end of January, *Ark Royal* put to sea and headed east with the battleship *Malaya* and battle-cruiser *Renown* for Operation *Picket*. On 2 February 1941 at 0558, a striking force of eight Swordfish flew off in poor but clearing weather, heading for the huge Santa Chiara d'Ula dam on Sardinia, the hydroelectric plant of which produced a great deal of electricity for the island. Unfortunately, it was cloudy and raining when the aircraft reached the coast, forcing all but one aircraft offshore to wait for better visibility — and the one pilot that proceeded lost his bearings in cloud and had to return without attacking. The rest attempted to find gaps in the cloud. One dodged through a gap between the clouds and a hill, and found his aircraft under a barrage of AA fire so dense it seemed utterly impossible to get through, so he jettisoned his torpedo and returned to the carrier. Another aircraft failed to find the dam. In the end, only four of the eight Swordfish attacked the dam, and caused some damage, but not enough to create a breach.

Four days after that, the heavy units of Force H assembled outside Genoa to carry out a bombardment of the docks (Operation *Result*). It had been hoped to catch at least part of the battle fleet in the harbour, but the ships had all moved on by the time Force H arrived. Furthermore, an opportunity to compound the damage done at Taranto was missed — the battleship *Caio Duilio* was in the dry dock under repair, but HMS *Renown*'s spotting aircraft failed to see it. Haze typical of the region may have been a contributory factor. *Ark Royal*, meanwhile, detached in order for her aircraft to carry out two missions — 14 aircraft set off to bomb the oil refinery at Leghorn, and four more laid mines in the harbour at La Spezia. Both proceeded relatively smoothly, with only one Swordfish shot down, though damage to the huge refinery was relatively light. Overall, Operations *Picket* and *Result* had not reaped the kinds of rewards they might have done, but the failure to achieve more can be attributed to dispersion of effort and planning than the aircraft and their crews.

On Malta, 830 Squadron was making a significant contribution. On 27 January 1941, the squadron staged an attack on a convoy that the Director of Naval Air Division (DNAD), Rear-Admiral Clement Moody, called a "classic" example of "perfect co-operation and execution". At 1035, a Short Sunderland reported a convoy off

Well-known image of Swordfish 'M' of 830 Squadron demonstrating the black colour scheme and long-range tank fitted in the rear cockpit. This squadron carried out a campaign of night anti-shipping strikes from Malta.

Lampedusa, and seven Swordfish escorted by two Fulmars were dispatched from Hal Far less than an hour later. It took nearly two hours to reach the target, which consisted of two merchant ships escorted by an armed merchantman. The force attacked out of the sun, splitting into three groups — the leader, the only Swordfish carrying bombs, attacked alone, dive-bombing the escort vessel with 250lb bombs, while the remainder split into two sub-flights, each attacking one of the merchant ships with a torpedo. The first of these was estimated to be around 7,500 tons — a possible hit was recorded — and the second, around 4,000 tons — a definite hit being scored. The merchantman hit was the SS *Ingo*, a German steamer of 3,950 GRT. It broke in two and sank within 10 minutes. This was confirmed by the Sunderland, which had continued to shadow until the Swordfish arrived, and stayed to observe results of the attack. This was seen as such a model attack that details of it were circulated to FAA training units.

During the first two months of the year, 830 Squadron carried out seven missions, mostly at night, including armed reconnaissance, night bombing on shipping in port, and minelaying with diversionary bombing raids. Cunningham kept a close eye on the squadron's work, however, and while he considered the "attacks are satisfactory and show that 830 Squadron is being operated on the right lines", he felt that "in view of the large number of tempting targets passing within range, the number of attacks made is somewhat disappointing". This was, however, rather outside 830 Squadron's control. The sustained air raids on Malta's airfields hampered serviceability of aircraft, and the fact that operations had to be restricted to darkness because of the Swordfish's vulnerability to fighters during daylight. Even under these circumstances, the number of raids the squadron was able to stage increased as the year went on. There was only one raid in March and two in April, but then four in May, seven in

June and six in July. Many of these involved minelaying or attacking shipping in Tripoli harbour. Others were attacks on convoys or ships travelling alone that reconnaissance flights had reported.

In February, the Royal Navy's focus in the eastern Mediterranean was turning to Greece, which had been invaded by Italy the previous October. That month, the Greek army launched a new offensive with British support. The veteran HMS *Eagle* was, after the damage to *Illustrious*, once again the only carrier in the eastern basin, so it fell to her to escort a convoy from Port Said to Piraeus. Previous experience had proved that *Eagle* was too small, too slow and, being unarmoured, was rather too vulnerable in those waters. Moreover, she was overdue for a refit. The old carrier had to hold the line until a replacement was available.

Back in December 1940, a new Illustrious-class carrier, HMS *Formidable*, had commissioned, and with the withdrawal of *Illustrious* for repairs, she was dispatched to the Mediterranean with her two TSR squadrons, 826 and 829. These units were both equipped with the newer Fairey Albacore, with which the FAA was now gradually replacing the Swordfish. However, deliveries of Albacores were still slow, so 829 Squadron had to partially revert to Swordfish to make good its losses. Indeed, supplies of Swordfish were picking up again. The first 'Blackfish', as Swordfish built by Blackburn were colloquially known, V4288, was taken into the air by Fairey test pilot F.H. 'Freddie' Dixon on 1 December.

With *Formidable* now taking *Illustrious*' place in the Mediterranean Fleet, *Eagle* was finally free to withdraw, and passed through the Suez Canal on 13 April. Her aircraft disembarked to Port Sudan, where they joined efforts to liquidate the Italian Red Sea Flotilla at Massawa, Eritrea. This force threatened shipping heading for the Mediterranean via the Suez Canal. It had sortied several times, including in October 1940 when it attacked convoy BN 7, and most recently on 31 March/1 April, despite being somewhat short on fuel by this time. The flotilla was then made up of three, large, powerful Leone-class destroyers, three Sauro-class destroyers (an additional ship of this class having been lost in November), a squadron of MAS (motor torpedo) boats, and four submarines (of an original eight), and various auxiliary and smaller vessels.

On 2 April, the 824 and 813 Squadron crews at Port Sudan received a high-priority signal from Aden, warning that destroyers at Massawa were raising steam. In fact, the flotilla was preparing for a 'death ride' at the RN forces in Port Sudan, and would arrive by the following morning. The available Swordfish were armed with 250lb bombs, and an aircraft was sent off to reconnoitre at 0530 the next day. Commander Charles Keighly-Peach (known to all as 'K-P'), *Eagle*'s Commander Flying, with his observer, Warrant Officer Wallington, spotted three destroyers racing towards Port Sudan. He radioed for support and went into the attack, though he missed with his bombs. When more Swordfish reached the scene, Midshipman Sergeant aimed at the *Nazario Sauro* and scored a direct hit. Lieutenant Wellham straddled a destroyer he identified as *Tigre* with his bombs, possibly causing damage with the near-misses, and Sub-Lieutenant Suthers scored a direct hit on *Daniele Manin*.[28] The Swordfish may also have damaged *Pantera*, as she was run aground by her crew, as was *Tigre*. *Sauro* and *Manin* sank as a result of the bomb hits. Sources vary, but it appears *Cesare Battista*, the only other destroyer in the flotilla, was unable to join the sortie due to mechanical problems and was scuttled slightly later. The beached destroyers were bombarded to destruction by HMS *Kingston*. This effectively ended the Red Sea Flotilla as a force, and the surviving vessels were given orders to be scuttled or try to escape. *Eagle*'s Swordfish hurried things along by strafing a launch that had assisted in the scuttling of other vessels, and bombed the torpedo boat *Giovanni Acerbi*,[29] rendering her operationally useless, though she was able to be sunk as a blockship. Allied forces captured Massawa soon afterwards, and HMS *Kingston* presented *Eagle* with the ensign from *Pantera* in recognition of the role the Swordfish had played in stamping out the flotilla. *Eagle* then spent a short while hunting for a raider in the Indian Ocean, before rounding the Cape of Good Hope to take up station in the South Atlantic.

In March 1941, 815 Squadron moved temporarily from the Western Desert to Crete, where it carried out anti-shipping operations in support of the Allied defence of Greece. According to Cunningham, "This squadron was very well handled and was a serious menace to the enemy. A number of large ships were sunk or damaged by torpedoes and bombs at Valona, Durazzo and even Brindisi."[30] On 13 March, they sank a large cargo ship at Valona, Albania, the *Santa Maria* with torpedoes, and the next night an even larger vessel, the *Po* – unfortunately, this turned out to be a hospital ship, a fact which was not apparent in the dark. On 17 March, the squadron attacked and sank the large, seagoing torpedo boat *Andromeda* off Valona.

That month, the Government Code and Cypher School at Bletchley Park broke Italian naval codes in time to reveal that the Regia Marina was planning a sortie to prey on Allied convoys transporting troops to Greece. The Mediterranean Fleet slipped out of Alexandria at nightfall on 27 March to interpose itself between the Italian fleet (now under Admiral Iachino, after Campioni's removal). By the following morning, Iachino was aware that the Royal Navy knew the Italian fleet was out, so consolidated his forces, which had previously been in two groups. Iachino was, however, unaware that Cunningham had three battleships, believing just one was in the British line, and crucially, did not know that *Formidable* was present. Had he known either of these facts, it is likely the he would have withdrawn. As it was, the engagement that would become known as the Battle of Cape Matapan was about to begin.

Formidable was suffering from the perennial problem of RN carrier forces, a shortage of aircraft. There were only 27 available, four of which were Swordfish – *Formidable*'s standard complement was 36 aircraft, and she could carry up to 54 if outriggers and a deck park were used. With the 10 Albacores of 829 and 826 Squadrons (only half of which had long-range fuel tanks), these made up the reconnaissance and striking capability, as well as anti-submarine patrol. As a result, the aircrews and aircraft were to be somewhat overworked over the next couple of days: "most of the TSR crews averaged ten to twelve and a half hours in the air," *Formidable*'s CO, Captain Bisset, later wrote.[31]

At 0555 on the 28th, *Formidable* flew off four Albacores and a Swordfish to reconnoitre for the Italian fleet. At 0720, the most northerly of the aircraft sighted cruisers and destroyers, and 19 minutes later, the next most northerly aircraft confirmed the sighting. At 0805, the second aircraft reported battleships. A striking force of 826 Squadron Albacores was flown off at 0956, joined by a Swordfish to act as observer and shadower.

By this time, the Italian 3rd Division of cruisers, and those of Vice-Admiral Pridham-Wippell, had made contact, south of Crete. The striking force sighted enemy ships at 1058, just as the Italian battleship *Vittorio Veneto* came within range of the RN cruisers and opened fire. The Albacores did not score any hits, though they forced Iachino to turn away from Pridham-Wippell's cruisers. (The shadowing Swordfish, 'Duty J', successfully kept tabs on the *Vittorio Veneto*, but sadly none of that aircraft's reports was received.)

A second strike was prepared, made up of three Albacores and two Swordfish of 829 Squadron (including aircraft that had been engaged in reconnaissance earlier in the day), escorted by two Fulmars, and was ranged and launched at 1230. About two and a half hours later, they sighted *Vittorio Veneto* with her escorts and began working round to attack out of the sun. The leader of the Swordfish sub-flight, Lieutenant Osborn, finding his aircraft somewhat left behind by the faster Albacores, 'cut the corner' and dived down on the battleship's starboard quarter and dropped his torpedo, claiming a possible hit. The crucial blow is generally held to have been struck by the Albacore of Lieutenant-Commander Dalyell-Stead (who was killed in the attack), although it is not impossible that it was Osborn's torpedo that did the damage, as it was fitted with a 'duplex' head designed to explode beneath the hull rather than on contact with it – it was not unknown for duplex torpedoes to pass under the keel and explode on the other side of the ship from the attacking aircraft. Whichever torpedo it was, it wrecked the port propeller shafts and caused major flooding. The second strike returned at 1600, but there was daylight left for one more, if the aircraft could be readied. Six Albacores and two Swordfish flew off at 1730.

It was not just the Swordfish from *Formidable* in the air at this time, as *Warspite* sent her scouting aircraft up to spot for the guns. The machine flown by the indefatigable Petty Officer Rice carried fleet observer Lieutenant-Commander Bolt, who sent a steady stream of messages back to the fleet about the course and speed of *Vittorio Veneto*. So long did Rice remain on station that when the time came to return, he had insufficient fuel to reach Suda Bay. Naturally *Warspite* could not stop to recover the Swordfish so the only alternative was the highly unusual manoeuvre of recovering while underway, involving the floatplane taxiing alongside the ship at speed while the crane was connected to the slinging gear. This nerve-wracking escapade was achieved without a hitch.

Meanwhile, the battle had moved within range of 815 Squadron at Maleme, so two of its Swordfish took off armed with torpedoes, led by Lieutenant Torrens-Spence and his observer, Sub-Lieutenant Winter, who successfully located the Italian warships shortly before the strike from *Formidable* arrived. Consequently, all aircraft went in to the attack at around 1920, some having waited until the sun set to allow dusk to mask their approach.

By this time, searchlight beams and a fearsome AA barrage from the warships were filling the air. All the destroyers and cruisers had formed a screen around the damaged battleship, and the attacking aircraft were forced to divide and attack individually, leading to confusion over which ships they were targeting. Previous fleet actions had demonstrated the difficulty in distinguishing Italian battleships from cruisers, and it seems likely that some or all of the aircraft were actually attacking one of the latter. Somehow, despite the volume of flak and several near-collisions, all the aircraft made it out unscathed, and flew to Malame rather than return to the carrier in the dark. One hit on a heavy cruiser was observed – this turned out to be the *Pola*, which had received a single hit amidships on the starboard side, having had to stop to avoid a collision with another cruiser. Her captain is reported to have said, "I have never seen such courage as was displayed by the aircraft attacking me. It came in about five feet above the water under a withering fire at short range, and I can only describe it as an act of God."[32]

The torpedo hit immobilised the cruiser, killed all power and thus rendered the guns unusable. Iachino detached two other heavy cruisers to escort and assist her, and during the night, all three were attacked and sunk by Cunningham's battleships. The crippling of *Vittorio Veneto* and the sinking of three heavy cruisers (and two destroyers), both enabled by Fleet Air Arm torpedo bombers, made Cape Matapan a triumph for the Mediterranean Fleet second only to Taranto. Furthermore, it proved that the torpedo bomber was capable of the purpose the Royal Navy envisaged for it – damaging and slowing down enemy warships to enable the navy's own surface ships to catch up and deal the fatal blow. Although the naval authorities were disappointed at failing to sink *Vittorio Veneto* too, she was out of action until August.

Swordfish 'K' serial not marked) wearing the black distemper on lower surfaces adopted for night operations by squadrons including 815 NAS before the raid on Taranto in November 1940. The full-height fin flash and roundel in an aft position with code in front were characteristic of markings in use before September 1940. Note the flare containers beneath the wings – successful flare drops were an essential part of the victory at Taranto.

However, days later, Allied forces in the region were once again on the back foot. The counter-offensive against Italian forces in Greece was proving successful, but on 6 April, the German Wehrmacht joined the fight with an overwhelming assault.

The Swordfish of 815 Squadron undertook their only minelaying operation of the campaign on 13 April, when they flew to the southern Italian port of Brindisi to mine the harbour. They had flown to Eleusis to pick up the 'cucumbers' (as the mines were referred to) on 11 April and the original intention had been to mine the Albanian port at Durazzo (Durrës), but it had already been overrun by the time the operation could be carried out. Three days after the Brindisi run, they were employed transporting valuable mines and torpedoes off the Greek mainland to Maleme on Crete. Afterwards, the squadron transferred to Nicosia on Cyprus.

Formidable was heavily occupied during the retreat from Greece and the subsequent battle for Crete, though mostly in fighter defence, and the number of serviceable TSRs continued to dwindle. While returning from a dawn raid on Scarpanto, Junkers Ju 87 'Stuka' dive-bombers hunting merchant ships happened upon the carrier, attacked and scored two hits with 1,000kg bombs. As with *Illustrious*, *Formidable* would need dockyard work to make good the damage, taking her out of the equation in the Mediterranean, and she disembarked her aircraft at Alexandria before heading for the US for repairs.

During May, it had been established that the Vichy French regime was allowing German forces to stage through Syria, which France governed under a League of Nations mandate. This led to a decision to blockade the coast and raid airfields. In July, the remaining aircraft of 826 and 829 Squadrons joined 815 at Nicosia in support of the Syrian blockade, with eight Swordfish and three Albacores across the three squadrons.

At first, the two units from *Formidable* moved to a satellite aerodrome (which had been constructed by Royal Engineers in 10 days), while 815 continued to operate from Nicosia, but as the latter was being heavily and frequently bombed, they later also moved to the satellite. The composition of the squadrons was then arranged as 815 and 826 with four Swordfish each, and 829 with three Albacores. Facilities were rudimentary, there were no facilities for servicing torpedoes, and the lack of equipment (only two torpedo trollies and no mobile crane) made it impossible to arm a strike force quickly. The aircraft were fitted with torpedoes permanently, which helped to expedite rapid responses to reconnaissance reports, but caused problems if different depth settings were required, as these could not be changed without removing the torpedoes.

However, the FAA crews settled in quickly and soon a complementary relationship with the RAF Beaufighter and Blenheim squadrons was established, particularly with regard to reconnaissance — the Beaufighters could provide long-range reconnaissance quickly, even in areas defended by fighters, Blenheims could cover large areas of open sea, and the Swordfish and Albacores could carry out armed reconnaissance closer to the island, and were especially suitable in low visibility or at night. While one of the TSR squadrons was carrying out armed reconnaissance, the other two could be on standby as a striking force, one at readiness and the other available at longer notice.

On 2 July, a Swordfish of 815 Squadron spotted and attacked an armed trawler in Castel Irizzo harbour. The torpedo missed the trawler and blew up under a steam yacht, destroying it and some nearby sailing vessels.

Two French steamships, the *St Didier* and the *Qued Yquem*, were known to be attempting to run the blockade, so considerable efforts were made to locate and attack them. On 4 July, one of the dawn-patrol Swordfish spotted a likely ship near Cape Khelidonia. The pilot approached closely, so as to be sure of identifying the ship positively, as it was flying Turkish colours, waving at the crew as if in friendship. Fortunately for the Swordfish, the *St Didier*'s crew waved back — the Swordfish's crew had spotted a gun on the forecastle and a Breda machine gun on the stern. They also noticed that "the ship was loaded with war materials and had tanks and lorries stowed on deck". The pilot quickly turned towards the *St Didier* and launched his torpedo, which passed directly under the ship but its duplex-fuse warhead failed to explode.

The sighting was reported to Nicosia where the strike force, of three 826 Squadron Swordfish, was waiting. Unfortunately, one of their torpedoes was set to 26 feet, far too great a depth for *St Didier*, but as it would take too long to change there was little point in bringing it; therefore, just two aircraft left at 1230. They reached the ship at 1500 but scored no hits, so a further strike in two waves was launched, four 829 Squadron Albacores followed 15 minutes later by four 815 Squadron Swordfish. Two of the former scored direct hits on the transport vessel, which rapidly sank, so 815 Squadron returned with their torpedoes and bombs unexpended.

The French then made various attempts to get *Qued Yquem* through, but without success. A Swordfish on armed reconnaissance spotted it on 7 July and near-missed astern with a bomb, which persuaded the captain to turn back, staying out of range of the Swordfish from Cyprus. After this, the French concluded that it was too risky to try to force the blockade and gave up.

The operation of Swordfish at Nicosia was not

easy, and the maintenance crews had their work cut out. The Pegasus engines were noted to suffer from high temperatures and heavy oil consumption, and the aircraft were almost always operating at maximum load, putting considerable strain on the powerplants. Nevertheless, only once did an aircraft have to abandon a mission with engine trouble. Of the three squadrons, 826 and 815 withdrew to Egypt to rest and re-equip, while 829 took six Swordfish on charge and embarked on HMS *Formidable*, to provide anti-submarine cover while she crossed the Atlantic for dockyard repairs. *Formidable* entered the Suez Canal on 24 July 1941, after which no fleet carrier was present in the eastern Mediterranean until the autumn of 1944.

In August 1941, 815 Squadron returned to Dekheila and was largely re-equipped with Albacores, but retained two Swordfish with anti-surface vessel (ASV) Mk II — an early radar set.

Profiles

SWORDFISH K4190 PROTOTYPE

First prototype Fairey TSR II K4190 as it originally appeared in 1934, with anti-spin strakes on the rear fuselage, 'bumped' Townend ring and two-blade propeller.

Profiles

SWORDFISH MKI K5661 PRE-PRODUCTION

Second of three pre-production Swordfish K5661 of the Station Flight, RAF Gosport, as it appeared at a public display in 1936 delivering a demonstration torpedo attack on a land-going mock-up of a Nelson-class battleship.

Profiles

SWORDFISH MKI K5662 FLOATPLANE

The third of three pre-production Swordfish, K5662, was completed as a floatplane, in which guise it undertook manufacturers' trials at Fairey Hamble.

Profiles

SWORDFISH MKI K8351 FLOATPLANE

Swordfish Mk I floatplane K8351 '810' of 823 Squadron as it appeared in October 1937 with HMS *Glorious* in the Mediterranean.

Profiles

SWORDFISH MKI L2970 820 SQUADRON, BISMARCK

Mk I L9720 '4A' of 820 Squadron, HMS *Ark Royal*, in 1941. This was probably the aircraft flown by Lt Hunter during the attack on the *Bismarck*. Aircraft is in obsolete S1E scheme. Note the 'white wall' tyres. A photograph of this aircraft appears in Stuart Lloyd's *Fleet Air Arm Camouflage and Markings: Atlantic and Mediterranean Theatres 1937–41*.

Profiles

SWORDFISH MKI L7678 821X FLIGHT

Fairey-built Mk I L7678 '5G' of 821 Squadron in late 1940, around the time the squadron reduced to the six Swordfish of 821X Flight for transit to Malta aboard HMS *Argus*, of which this aircraft was one. Colours are the Temperate Sea Scheme adopted from June 1940, with Sky undersides and Dark Slate Grey/Extra Dark Sea Grey upper surfaces.

Profiles

SWORDFISH MKI P4127 820 SQUADRON, ATTACK ON SARDINIA

P4127 '4F' of 820 Squadron, HMS *Ark Royal*, as it took part in a raid on Cagliari, Sardinia, on 2 August 1940, when it was hit by AA fire and the pilot Lt Humphries forced to land. Colours are the S1E scheme of 1939-40, with Sky Grey undersides.

Profiles

SWORDFISH MKI P4154 815 SQUADRON, TARANTO

In late 1940, 815 Squadron aboard HMS *Illustrious* had painted its aircraft with a black distemper on the underside for night operations, and extended the upper camouflage colours down the side. P4154 '4M' was flown by Lt Swayne during the attack on the Italian Fleet at Taranto.

Profiles

SWORDFISH MKI V4367 FLOATPLANE

Blackburn-built Mk I floatplane V4367, the catapult aircraft for the battleship HMS *Malaya*, in autumn 1941.

Profiles

SWORDFISH MKI W5985 CHANNEL DASH

W5985 'K', The Swordfish of Sub-Lt Ralph Wood and his crew, Sub-Lt Fuller-Wright and LA Wheeler of 825 Squadron, during the ill-fated attack on *Scharnhorst* and *Gneisenau* from RAF Manston, 12 February 1942, known as the 'Channel Dash'. All three were killed when their Swordfish was shot down by fighters.

Profiles

SWORDFISH MKII HS545 BATTLE OF THE ATLANTIC

Mk II HS545 'B' of 824 Squadron in September/October 1944, when the squadron undertook convoy protection in the Atlantic and Russian convoys. The predominantly white scheme was adopted for trade protection carriers in late 1942, and as seen here was evidently applied over the old Temperate Sea Scheme, now showing through in large areas.

Profiles

SWORDFISH MK II LS226, 836 SQUADRON

LS226/H4, which was flown by Sub-Lt Meen, Sub-Lt Ryley and LA Cribb, during a search for a missing Wellington in February 1944. No. 836 Squadron supplied crews for Merchant Aircraft Carriers (MAC ships).

Profiles

SWORDFISH MKII LS454 CEYLON

Mk II LS454, one of a handful of Swordfish operated in the fleet requirements role by 733 Squadron, RNAS China Bay, in 1945, wearing all-over aluminium dope and Eastern Fleet small blue-white roundels and blue-white fin-flash.

Profiles

SWORDFISH MKII NE951 MAC SHIP

Swordfish Mk II NE951 'S1' as operated by 860 Dutch Squadron from May 1944 aboard the Dutch-crewed Merchant Aircraft Carrier *Gadila*. The squadron and ship's Dutch connections are marked with an orange triangle on the fin, complemented by strictly non-standard orange codes.

Profiles

SWORDFISH MKIII NF410 119 SQUADRON RAF

Swordfish Mk III NF410 'NH-F' of 119 Squadron, RAF, flying from Knokke-le-Zoute in Belgium between February and May 1945 on night anti-shipping patrol and strike. This aircraft wore Donald Duck nose art.

Profiles

SWORDFISH POSTWAR MKII G-AJVH

Mk II LS326 was acquired by Fairey Aviation in 1946 and registered G-AJVH, after a while being given a striking livery of Fairey house colours, blue and silver. The aircraft was flown in these colours until 1959 when it reverted to wartime camouflage for the film *Sink the Bismarck!*.

7

SINK THE *BISMARCK*!

POWERFUL KRIEGSMARINE capital ships and heavy cruisers had been a cause of worry to the Admiralty since the beginning of the war, and considerable thought was given to how one might be countered if it attempted to break into the Atlantic to prey on the vital convoys keeping Britain from starvation. Hunting groups of warships would be required, and "The decisive element of any such combination would be the aircraft carrier because she would be the means of locating the enemy and reducing his speed below that of our forces".[33]

On 19 May 1941, the worst fears of the Admiralty were confirmed when the battleship *Bismarck*, then the largest and most powerful in the world, left port heading for the Atlantic with the cruiser *Prinz Eugen*.

All available RN warships were immediately diverted to the hunt. This included HMS *Victorious*, the newest Illustrious-class carrier, which was then attached to the Home Fleet, and had been waiting in the Clyde for a troop convoy to assemble. She had commissioned a mere 10 days before HMS *Hood* was sunk, and her squadrons were incomplete — indeed, the only operational aircraft aboard were nine Swordfish of 825 Squadron, and six Fulmars for the hastily assembled pilots making up a 'scratch' 800 Squadron.

Although 825 Squadron had been operational for some time, many of its aircrews were recent replacements, and the squadron as constituted had never carried out a practice torpedo attack. *Victorious* sailed with the bulk of the Home Fleet on 22 May. Approaching from the other direction, and at the other end of the experience scale, was *Ark Royal* with Force H.

In the morning on the 24th, *Bismarck* was intercepted by HMS *Hood* and HMS *Prince of Wales*, but sank the former and damaged the latter, forcing her to withdraw. *Bismarck* was subsequently shadowed by *Prince of Wales* and the cruisers HMS *Norfolk* and *Suffolk*. Admiral Tovey, in overall command, ordered *Victorious* to close and fly off a strike to try and slow *Bismarck* down. Captain Bovell considered that the best chance of success lay in sending out as large a strike as possible, so launched all nine of his Swordfish. They flew off at 2210, led by Lieutenant-Commander E.R. Esmonde.

Visibility was poor but the Swordfish had an advantage FAA TSRs had not previously enjoyed. Three of the machines were fitted with ASV. This, in conjunction with excellent navigation, enabled 825 Squadron to locate the battleship at 2330, despite thickening cloud. Esmonde altered course to try to approach the battleship from ahead, but in doing so lost contact. Undeterred, the Swordfish continued circling, and found HMS *Norfolk*, which directed them back towards *Bismarck* via signal lamp, and shortly afterwards, the ASV once again picked up a contact.

The squadron dipped beneath the cloud, only to find that the return the ASV had shown was not their target but a US Coastguard cutter that had blundered into the middle of the biggest naval chase of the war. Unfortunately, *Bismarck* was only six miles away and spotted the Swordfish as they exited the cloud, losing them the benefit of surprise, and alerting the AA gunners. The Swordfish crews pressed home their attack despite a heavy barrage and the increasingly poor weather. Sub-Lieutenant Houston got lost in cloud but the remaining eight all got through to launch their torpedoes, and remarkably, no Swordfish were shot down.

Despite their lack of recent experience, 825 Squadron carried out something close to the classic simultaneous attack by several sub-flights with skill and dash. Esmonde flew up the port side, attempting to work round to attack on the starboard bow with the intention that the other two members of his sub-flight would attack the port bow. An AA hit on his starboard aileron persuaded Esmonde to go right into the attack, and he and Sub-Lieutenant Thompson dropped on the port bow, while Lieutenant Maclean was separated from Esmonde on the way in and attacked the port beam slightly earlier than the other two. *Bismarck* was now manoeuvring hard, and managed to avoid these three torpedoes. The second sub-flight, led by Lieutenant Gick, was coming in from starboard, but Gick broke off as he was unhappy with his position. Staying low, he led his sub-flight around for another approach.

In the meantime, the third sub-flight led by Lieutenant Pollard (without Houston) was attacking on the port quarter, having taken a longer approach through less intense AA fire to launch from a good position.

The battleship had so far managed to avoid all the torpedoes launched at it, and the AA guns were maintaining a withering fire, but just after the third sub-flight had attacked, Gick's machine, 5F,[34] followed by Garthwaite and Jackson, emerged from the murk on the port bow and launched at close range. A torpedo struck home, exploding amidships on the battleship's armour belt.

"A tremendous shudder ran through the hull and a towering column of water rose at *Bismarck*'s side," a crewmember recounted.[35]

Admiral Tovey wrote in his dispatch to the Admiralty that "This attack, by a squadron so lately embarked in a new carrier, in unfavourable weather conditions, was magnificently carried out and reflects the greatest credit on all concerned," adding, "There can be little doubt that the hit was largely responsible for the *Bismarck* finally being brought to action and sunk."[36]

The exact effect of 825 Squadron's torpedo strike will probably now never be known. It was, however, either that or the vigorous evasive manoeuvres that the battleship was subjected to, which caused further damage. Temporary repairs secured over the damage caused by *Prince of Wales* in the earlier battle were shaken loose, and the adjacent spaces began to flood again. Boiler room No. 2, which had been partially flooded, now had to be completely abandoned. This loss and the weight of water taken on board contributed to a slight reduction in *Bismarck*'s speed that would later prove crucial.[37]

The attack had proved beyond doubt the value of ASV, and had also vindicated Bovell's somewhat risky call to send every single Swordfish (although he was lucky in this that the weather obviated the need for an anti-submarine patrol, and no reconnaissance to find the target was necessary).

Despite this, later that night *Bismarck* succeeded in shaking off the pursuing warships. Admiral Lütjens, unaware that he was no longer being tailed, sent several long radio messages back to Berlin which were picked up by Allied Direction Finding (D/F) stations. However, rather than help the Home Fleet locate the *Bismarck*, this

A Swordfish fitted with ASV (anti surface-vessel) Mk II radar, as indicated by the aerials on the interplane struts, about to take off from a carrier. ASV-equipped Swordfish proved a great advantage during the attacks on the *Bismarck* due to the poor visibility and thick cloud.

development contrived to throw Tovey further off the scent. The bearings were calculated incorrectly on his flagship, and as a result he positioned his warships to intercept *Bismarck* returning to Germany through the Iceland–Faroes gap rather than, as she was, proceeding to Brest. By the time it was realised where *Bismarck* was heading, hours had been lost, the distance had opened considerably, and with the fuel available it was unlikely Tovey's ships would be able to catch up before the battleship was under the protection of aircraft from occupied France.

There was one last hope of defeating *Bismarck* before she reached safety: Force H and the Swordfish aboard HMS *Ark Royal*. If one of these could cause enough damage to the battleship to slow her down, it was possible that the pursuing Home Fleet could still catch and overwhelm her.

Contact was re-established in the morning of 26 May, with *Bismarck* heading to eastward approximately 680 nautical miles from Brest. First, a Consolidated Catalina of RAF Coastal Command located the battleship, and shortly afterwards, Swordfish on reconnaissance from *Ark Royal*, steaming north from Gibraltar with Force H also made a sighting, 25 miles to the east of the position given by the Catalina. *Ark Royal* immediately began preparations to launch a strike. This nearly ended in disaster, as has been well documented, as the CinC had detached the cruiser HMS *Sheffield* to shadow *Bismarck*, and the message had not got through to the *Ark Royal* aircrews who believed that *Bismarck* was the only ship in the area. The 14-aircraft strike was flown off at 1315, ASV indicating a ship around 20 nautical miles from the last position they had been given. The Swordfish attacked, and launched 11 torpedoes at the target before it was realised that the ship was not *Bismarck* but a RN cruiser. Somewhat with their tails between their legs, the pilots of 818 and 820 Squadrons returned to *Ark Royal*.

They had, however, learned a valuable lesson. *Sheffield* had ably avoided many of the torpedoes, but was aided in this by a number of them clearly detonating early. The fault was correctly identified as the 'duplex pistols' in the torpedo warheads. As noted earlier, the Fleet Air Arm had begun to change the traditional contact pistols in its torpedoes early in the war for a magnetic fuse, known as the duplex coil rod. The advantage in this was that it could be set to run at a depth below that of the ship being targeted and explode directly under the hull, avoiding any armour and breaking its back through 'water hammer' effect. 'Duplex' torpedoes had worked spectacularly at Taranto, convincing the RN of their superiority. However, the circumstances at Taranto had suited the duplex head — somewhat ironically, as the RN initially considered it less likely to work well in restricted waters. In open water, distinctly mixed results had been experienced, with either early detonations or a failure to explode even on a perfect run. In reality, problems had been noted as early as the Norwegian campaign, but the precise reason for the failures was not clear. In the rough waters of the North Atlantic, the problems with the duplex pistol seemed more acute than ever.

A second strike was prepared, with torpedoes set to detonate on contact. This meant it was less likely that catastrophic damage could be inflicted, balanced against the greater likelihood of the torpedo working effectively.

The weather at this time was not easy for flying. The wind was strong, force 6, and a severe swell running. Four Swordfish each from 810 and 818 Squadrons, and seven from 820 Squadron, took off at 1910 and formed up in two groups, line-astern. They were sub-divided into six sub-flights aiming to carry out a simultaneous attack.

This time, the Swordfish were detailed to rendezvous with *Sheffield* first, making the crossing below the cloud. Once the cruiser had been sighted, the striking force climbed to 6,000 feet, noting that there was 7/10 cloud coverage, with cloud from 2,000 feet to 5,000 feet, conditions described as "ideal for torpedo attack".[38] At 2035 the force took its departure from *Sheffield*, after the cruiser had passed on bearing and distance to *Bismarck*. As the Swordfish approached, however, the cloud began to thicken and the aircraft ran into a thick mass with its base at just 700 feet and its top anywhere from 6,000 feet to 10,000 feet. Many aircraft became separated while trying to climb through it. The first sub-flight (Lieutenant-Commander Coode leading) dived down through the cloud where they estimated *Bismarck* to be, and found themselves four miles from the battleship. Coode popped back into the cloud to approach, and emerged to *Bismarck*'s port, then went into the attack, followed by an aircraft from the third sub-flight which had lost its leader, which helpfully reported one possible hit from the three aircraft, apparently about two-thirds back along the hull.

The second sub-flight, led by Lieutenant Godfrey-Faussett, lost touch with the first (and one of its own aircraft) and climbed to 9,000 feet in an effort to rise above the cloud — to no avail, as ice began to form on the Swordfish. The leader located the battleship by ASV, and dived through the cloud to emerge on the starboard beam, experiencing "intense and accurate AA fire from the first moment of sighting until out of range".[39] The third Swordfish, flown by Sub-Lieutenant Beale, returned to *Sheffield* for a new bearing, and tried again later.

The third sub-flight was made up of two aircraft, which became separated in cloud and attacked with other sub-flights.

The fourth sub-flight also found their aircraft starting to ice up in the cloud, and descended through a gap in the cloud, meeting up with the second aircraft from the third sub-flight, in time to see the second group attack. They circled *Bismarck*'s stern, dived through a patch of low cloud, and all aircraft launched simultaneously.

Sub-flight no. 5, made up of two aircraft, became separated and the leader, Lieutenant

Swordfish fly off HMS *Ark Royal*, viewed from the cruiser HMS *Sheffield* in 1941. *Ark Royal* and *Sheffield,* as part of Force H, played a crucial role in the sinking of the *Bismarck*, after *Ark Royal*'s aircraft accidentally attempted to torpedo *Sheffield*.

Owensmith, dipped in and out of cloud in order to work round to the starboard bow, withdrew to five miles distance and came in clipping the wavetops, to drop just outside 1,000 yards. Sub-Lieutenant Dixon, meanwhile, could not find a way through the intense AA barrage, and jettisoned his torpedo before returning to *Ark Royal*.

Sub-Lieutenant Beale from the second sub-flight had, meanwhile, found *Sheffield* and received a new bearing. He set off once again and made his attack, alone, from the port bow – his crew saw the torpedo hit on the port side, amidships.

The sixth sub-flight was also compelled to return to *Sheffield* for a bearing, and by the time they returned to *Bismarck*, the AA barrage was so heavy and accurate, they could not get close. One pilot launched at the battleship at extreme range, the other turned back and jettisoned his torpedo.

Once again, not a single Swordfish had been shot down, which seemed little short of miraculous. Four aircraft took damage from splinters thrown out by the heavy flak, and 4C of 820 Squadron was written off, with 175 holes counted. Two of the three crewmembers of that aircraft were wounded by splinters too, pilot Sub-Lieutenant Swanton and TAG Leading Airman Seager.

The Swordfish returned, certain of having scored at least two and possibly three hits, but unsure of how much damage had been inflicted. A reconnaissance Swordfish shadowing the battleship soon revealed the truth. *Bismarck* had been seen to turn in two full circles. She was out of control. Suddenly, what had seemed like a vanishingly small chance of preventing the battleship reaching safety was now a near certainty.

What *Ark Royal*'s Swordfish crews were only dimly aware of at the time was that a torpedo, probably the one launched by Sub-Lieutenant

Swordfish 'C' of 789 Squadron over the South Atlantic between September 1942 and July 1943. This squadron was a fleet requirements unit based at Wingfield, South Africa.

J.W.C. 'Jock' Moffatt of 818 Squadron, had caused severe damage at the battleship's stern and rendered her impossible to steer. Some confusion has arisen over which side the torpedo struck, but Coode's sub-flight attacked from port, and research by the International Naval Research Organization indicates that the torpedo struck on the port side — probably just above the port rudder. The confusion may have arisen from the following aircraft of the third sub-flight mistakenly indicating that the hit they saw — almost certainly the fatal one — was on the starboard side.

The torpedo caused catastrophic damage. The force of the explosion doubtless damaged the rudder itself, but more importantly, caused the long, overhanging stern to 'whip', further wrecking the steering gear inside the hull, ironically exacerbated by the rigid armoured box the steering motors were contained within, and jamming the rudders in a turn to port. The interior decks and bulkheads were savaged by the blast, hampering any efforts to repair the damage, although in truth it is unlikely the repair teams would have been able to restore steering with the facilities available, even if they had not been under pursuit. Although one of the rudders was eventually freed, the other was beyond repair. On the morning of 27 May, *Bismarck* was surrounded by Royal Navy capital ships, and from that point, the end was never in doubt. After an increasingly one-sided battle, *Bismarck* sank 464 nautical miles west of Brest.

The Swordfish from *Victorious* and especially *Ark Royal*, had fulfilled in a textbook manner the role intended for them from the aircraft's creation, as at Cape Matapan, to cause sufficient damage to an enemy warship to slow it down and weaken it, so it could be caught and brought to battle by the 'big gun' warships of the Royal Navy.

The risk to vital sea lanes from the *Bismarck* herself was over, but the raider threat remained. Further ships were either at sea or capable of putting to sea, and several of the support vessels that aimed to resupply raiders at sea were still at large. Most urgently, the cruiser *Prinz Eugen* had detached from *Bismarck* before the final battles and remained undetected. As it was, she was heading to Brest with engine defects, but the Admiralty was unaware of this and detailed *Victorious* and *Ark Royal* to search for her. Meanwhile *Eagle*, having withdrawn from the Mediterranean Fleet the previous month, took up station further west with the cruiser *Dunedin*.

On 4 June, a patrolling Swordfish from *Victorious* spotted the supply ship *Gonzenheim* 200 miles north of the Azores, where she had been waiting for *Bismarck*. The ship's position was passed on to hunting surface units, but before they could close with the ship, her crew scuttled her.

Two days later, one of *Eagle*'s Swordfish spotted a steamship flying Norwegian colours, which altered course and increased speed on seeing the aircraft. The behaviour and description of the ship passed on by the Swordfish crew suggested that its identity might be false. *Dunedin* was refuelling and could not respond to the report, so a searching force of bomb-armed Swordfish was sent out to re-locate the vessel, which was in fact the supply ship *Elbe*.

Aircraft 'Duty B', flown by Midshipman Hughes, found the suspect vessel and sent a signal to the rest of the force. Unfortunately, only two other aircraft received this and they were too far away. Hughes continued to shadow the steamer for over two hours until his fuel began to run low. At 1700, as no other aircraft had arrived to support him, Hughes attempted to stop the ship by firing a machine gun across the bows. This had no effect, so he attacked with his two 500lb bombs, which detonated 20 feet from the ship's port side, then returned to *Eagle*, arriving with barely 10 minutes' worth of fuel left.

Meanwhile *Eagle*, aware that no other Swordfish were able to assist Hughes, had sent out a second striking force. This arrived 25 minutes after Hughes had begun his attack, and found the ship on fire and being abandoned, the crew having attempted to scuttle her. The Swordfish eagerly assisted, scoring a hit with a 500lb bomb which blew out a cargo hatch, increased the fires and caused the ship to take on a list and sink by the stern. *Eagle* sent out aircraft the next day to search for the ship's boats, but found only debris. (Two weeks later, the armed boarding vessel HMS *Hilary* rescued 19 survivors.)

That day, however, *Prinz Eugen* reached Brest, having successfully dodged over 100 RN warships looking for her. *Ark Royal* and *Victorious* were ordered to cease their searches, and return to their parent fleets.

Eagle remained on station and on the 15th, Hughes was once again carrying out an armed reconnaissance and spotted a tanker — in fact another raider supply vessel, the *Lothringen*. He signalled for it to stop and when that failed, shot across the bows with a machine gun. The Swordfish immediately found itself under return fire from a machine gun on the tanker, which struck the fuselage and wings. Undaunted, Hughes dive-bombed *Lothringen* and scored two hits with his 250lb bombs, machine-gunning the ship for good measure. Hughes saw the tanker circling and training an oily wake before he returned to *Eagle*.

A second shadowing Swordfish was dispatched, and arrived to find the tanker flying white flags, and the crew waving a white sheet from the bridge. It appeared preparations were being made to lower the boats, so the pilot, Sub-Lieutenant Camidge, and crew machine-gunned them to prevent them being launched, thus avoiding a repeat of the *Elbe* situation. In the meantime, a strike force of three Swordfish had been flown off in case it was needed. Lieutenant Wellham was one of the pilots, and described what they found:

> As we approached, we were astonished to find a large, modern ship, stopped and wearing no ensign, with our shadowing Swordfish circling around her, at a height of some 500 feet ... It transpired that the captain of *Lothengen* [sic], on sighting

our Swordfish, had decided there was no future in arguing with aircraft and had surrendered. We explained the situation to *Eagle* by radio, asking for a relief shadower to home *Dunedin*, who was already on her way. We then made a number of 'show off' passes over the German ship, at a low altitude, to keep her frightened by a good view of our bombs, then turned back to our ship ... When we landed on *Eagle* we found an unexpected amount of interest in our rather tame episode. Apparently, it was the first time on record that a ship had surrendered to an aircraft.

Indeed, even though *Lothringen* had been hit by two 250lb bombs, and scuttling charges had been set, the tanker was ready to sail within six hours — a rare case of naval aircraft taking a prize!

Eagle was long overdue for a boiler clean, but this had been postponed when *Bismarck* broke out into the Atlantic. Nevertheless, she continued to operate in the South Atlantic at the request of the local commander, as a German raider had been reported in the area. Sadly, on 20 September, a fire broke out in her hangar when a pyrotechnic ignited during maintenance. All but four Swordfish were rendered unserviceable. Air patrols continued even with this reduced complement, but the following day, the old carrier's ailing machinery experienced yet another fault, which reduced her speed still further. (She was already operating at reduced speed due to a defect with her evaporators and the state of her boilers.) She put into Freetown, then sailed for the UK, arriving at the Clyde on 26 October.

The focus of the war was changing, and after the excitement of the *Bismarck* hunt, the opportunities for attacking enemy warships at sea or in port would begin to diminish. With the departure of HMS *Formidable*, the Mediterranean Fleet would no longer have an aircraft carrier for much of the remainder of the war. The Swordfish in that part of the theatre would all be land-based, some in Egypt supporting the Western Desert campaign, and of course 830 Squadron on Malta, doing its best to hamper shipping supplying the Afrika Korps.

The two squadrons left at Dekheila after the Syrian campaign, 815 and 826, were placed under RAF control to support operations in Libya from 25 June 1941. Now 815 NAS was chiefly equipped with Albacores, but still had two ASV-fitted Swordfish which were employed on anti-submarine patrols off the coast. One of these, V4707, attacked *U-652* off Sollum in April 1942, sharing the claim for its sinking with an RAF Blenheim. In the Western Desert, 826 also had a mix of Swordfish and Albacores, replacing the last of its Swordfish in September. They were joined by 821 Squadron, which had reformed with six Swordfish in July after the original unit had been absorbed into 815 NAS. The three TSR squadrons operated in support of the Eighth Army, and became specialised in night bombing and target-marking.

In the western Mediterranean, *Ark Royal* returned that May and was chiefly occupied with operations to supply aircraft to Malta, including supplemental Swordfish for 830 Squadron during Operation *Substance* in July, with the Albacores of 828 Squadron to reinforcing the veteran unit. The two squadrons were merged, for operational purposes, into the Royal Navy Air Squadron, Malta, though they retained their own 'number plates'. Operations tended to take place with a mixture of Swordfish and Albacores. The Swordfish equipped with ASV acted as 'pathfinders', navigating for a striking force and then dropping flares to illuminate the target. Missions involved anti-shipping strikes at night, raids on shipping and dockside facilities at ports in Sicily, Italy and North Africa, and minelaying.

In August, *Ark Royal*'s Swordfish took part in a somewhat bizarre operation as a diversion to HMS *Manxman* laying minefields off Livorno and a fast convoy of two transports returning empty from Malta. Operation *Mincemeat* (not to be confused with the later disinformation operation of the same name) involved various elements, one of which was an attack on the cork forests of Tempio, on the island of Sardinia. On 24 August at 0255, 10 Swordfish from 825, 810 and 816 Squadrons took off armed with incendiary bombs. It was a clear, starlit night, and the island's blackout was not being well observed, so it was straightforward for the aircraft to find their way. Cork forests and a factory were left well alight. Newspaper reports trumpeted the success: "The Admiral, in a congratulatory signal, summed up the success of the raid as follows: 'I estimate that there was enough burnt cork to give every Nazi a Hitler moustache.' Several hundred tons of incendiary and high explosive bombs were dropped in an area of 16 miles of forests."[40]

While cork was indeed a reasonably important substance to the war effort, the intention seems to have been to divert Axis attention from the minelaying as spectacularly as possible. In fact, the Regia Marina was aware that the RN was at sea, and Iachino sallied forth with two battleships and several cruisers, which RAF reconnaissance reported to Somerville, leading *Ark Royal* to ready a strike force. The fleets groped about for a while, but failed to find each other and both disengaged to return to port.

Operation *Halberd* the following month was the latest in a string of operations to supply Malta with provisions and arms. On 27 September, Force H received reconnaissance reports that Italian battleships and cruisers were at sea, and only 70–75 miles from the convoy. Two Swordfish were flown off to shadow the fleet while a strike force was readied. However, the Italian ships reversed course and the striking force failed to locate them. The escort was ordered to return to the convoy.

Another convoy followed the next month, but as this time the Italian fleet did not venture out of port, the Swordfish were chiefly occupied with anti-submarine duties. Operation *Perpetual*, in November, looked to be a repeat of the same.

Since September, however, increasing numbers of German U-boats had passed through the Straits of Gibraltar to reinforce the Regia Marina's submarines, and began operating from Salamis. A report that submarines were in the area was followed by various sonar contacts from the escorting destroyers, although nothing was sighted by the six Swordfish *Ark Royal* had flown off on anti-submarine patrol. At 1541 on 13 November, *Ark Royal* was struck by a torpedo in the starboard beam. She quickly took on a list, which was not opposed by counter-flooding, the appropriate regulation at the time stating, "It is the object of the enemy to let water into the ship, and he should not be helped by letting it in unnecessarily."[41] The carrier had been operating aircraft when she was struck, so a number of her aircraft were in the air. Many more were stuck on the deck and in the hangar, and went to the bottom when the carrier sank the next morning, within sight of Gibraltar. The Swordfish that were in flight headed to North Front, where it was determined that there were enough aircraft to retain 812 Squadron while 816 and 825 would have to be disbanded through lack of aircraft, though most of the crews in fact survived.

With the loss of *Ark Royal*, another carrier was badly needed in the western Mediterranean, and once again it was down to the veteran HMS *Eagle* to step into the breach. Her two Swordfish squadrons, 813 and 824, re-embarked at the end of January 1942 and the carrier sailed for Gibraltar the following month as part of the escort for convoy WS16. As in the second half of 1941, the focus on operations was on protecting supply convoys and fighter deliveries from air attack rather than the increasingly wary Italian battle fleet, so most of *Eagle*'s Swordfish were displaced to carry more fighters. A small cadre of the biplanes was retained on each cruise for anti-submarine patrol, the 'duty' flight alternating between 813 and 824, while the rest remained at North Front. Fighter delivery operations took place in March and May, the latter (Operation *Bowery*) also involving the US Navy (USN) carrier USS *Wasp*.

8

SLAUGHTER IN THE CHANNEL

Back in home waters, the Admiralty had become increasingly concerned that the two Kriegsmarine battle-cruisers *Scharnhorst* and *Gneisenau* would attempt to sail back to Germany from Brest, possibly via the English Channel. In January 1942, 825 Squadron, formerly of *Victorious*' and *Ark Royal*'s air groups, reformed at Lee-on-Solent with nine Swordfish Mk Is, under the command of Lieutenant-Commander Esmonde who had led the strike from *Victorious* on *Bismarck* the previous May. On 4 February, the squadron moved to Manston in Kent as part of Operation *Fuller*, the RN's planned response to a passage via the Channel — although eight days later, a detachment of six Swordfish left for Machrihanish in Scotland, leaving six machines at Manston. What followed would become known as the 'Channel Dash'.

On 11 February, members of 825 Squadron and RAF units at Manston held a party to celebrate Esmonde receiving the Distinguished Service Order, which he had been awarded for his role in the *Bismarck* attacks. As they toasted their CO, the Swordfish crews had little idea that the battle-cruisers were casting off to slip out of port. Due to various mishaps and failures in organisation, the squadron of ships (including the heavy cruiser *Prinz Eugen* and numerous destroyers as well as the two battle-cruisers) had passed Cherbourg by the time British reconnaissance happened upon them, and problems with reporting meant it was late morning on 12 February before the officer in command of Operation *Fuller*, Admiral Ramsay, was made aware.[42]

The main reason 825 Squadron had been recruited to Operation *Fuller* was for the Swordfish's ability to make night torpedo attacks, the skills and tactics of which had been perfected in the first two years of war. However, the opportunity to attack the Kriegsmarine ships at night had passed. It was now broad daylight, but the Bristol Beaufort torpedo bombers of Coastal Command were not yet in a position to attack, having been caught in inappropriate locations, and RAF bombers were loaded with the wrong bombs. Yet by midday, the ships were nearing the Strait of Dover, and in fact they had passed Dover by the time any attempt to attack them at all was made.

The Swordfish were then the only aircraft directly available that could mount an attack. Admiral Ramsay discussed the almost suicidal risks with the First Sea Lord, Sir Dudley Pound, who told him "The navy will attack the enemy whenever and wherever he is to be found."[43] There was still some hope that with a heavy fighter escort, the torpedo bombers might get through. They were detailed to depart with their escort no later than 1225, though yet more organisational failings meant that this time came and went, and of the five fighter squadrons assigned to escort the Swordfish, only one (72 Squadron) had arrived. The weather was worsening and Esmonde decided to depart, the Swordfish in two 'sub-flights' of three. It was stated at the later board of inquiry into the operation that the convention typically used by the RAF was not to depart until the full escort had arrived. However, Esmonde would have been conscious that every minute saw the battle-cruisers further away, and the low speed of the Swordfish meant that time was of the essence — if the warships could reach the shallow waters among the sandbanks northeast of Calais, a torpedo attack would be less likely to succeed. Moreover, the longer it took the Swordfish to approach the target, the more exposed they would be to fighter attack and AA fire. The board of inquiry heard that Esmonde was desperate to leave as soon as possible, but agreed with his reasoning.

No more than around 12 minutes from departure, the Spitfires spotted the warships, immediately becoming tangled up with the Luftwaffe fighter umbrella and unable to prevent Messerschmitt Bf 109s and Focke-Wulf Fw 190s from mauling the Swordfish. The first sub-flight was set upon by fighters, and all three aircraft were damaged, but pressed on, momentarily left alone by the fighters. As Esmonde approached the destroyer screen, he "encountered a withering anti-aircraft fire, which shot away most of his port wing, but was observed to regain control of his aircraft, straighten up and fly on steadily towards the battle-cruisers".[44] Esmonde zeroed in on the *Prinz Eugen*, but before could reach the dropping point, his aircraft was attacked by a fighter again, and "crashed into the sea". All three crewmembers were killed.

The two remaining aircraft of the sub-flight continued, though they were also under attack. Sub-Lieutenant Rose had already been wounded by this time, and his gunner Leading Airman Johnson, killed. Rose aimed at *Gneisenau* and launched his torpedo at long range, but unsurprisingly it missed. The Swordfish was crippled by this point, and Rose ditched in the sea, having to be helped into the dinghy by observer Sub-Lieutenant Lee. The third aircraft, flown by Sub-Lieutenant Kingsmill, was hit by a cannon shell that wounded him and his observer, Lieutenant Samples, but went round again after failing to line up on a target satisfactorily the first time, passing a second time over the destroyer screen with its murderous AA barrage. Kingsmill launched his torpedo at *Prinz Eugen* from 2,000 yards, but the cruiser evaded it. The Swordfish was now on fire, and Kingsmill ditched close to some British motor torpedo boats. It would have been scant consolation that Kingsmill's TAG, Petty Officer Bunce, shot down a Luftwaffe fighter with his Vickers machine gun.

Little is known about the ordeal of the second sub-flight, as there were no survivors, and indeed, only one body from the nine aircrew was ever recovered. The aircraft of Lieutenant Thompson, observer Sub-Lieutenant Parkinson and TAG Petty Officer Tapping; Sub-Lieutenant Wood, Sub-Lieutenant Wright and Petty Officer Wheeler; Sub-Lieutenant Bligh, Sub-Lieutenant Benyon, and Petty Officer Smith were all shot down. It is unclear if they launched their torpedoes or not. They simply flew into oblivion.

Esmonde received a posthumous Victoria Cross, while the other aircrews killed received posthumous Mentions in Dispatches. The surviving officers were awarded the DSO, and Bunce received the Conspicuous Gallantry Medal.

All in all, it was a shocking and senseless waste. The weakness of the Swordfish in daylight, against modern fighters, was well known by the Fleet Air Arm, and the fate of 825 Squadron's crews can have come as little surprise. While the Swordfish clearly still had much to offer, particularly in its proven ability to act at night and in poor weather, it was becoming too vulnerable against battle fleets in daylight. The misconception under which the Swordfish had been created, that the fleet's main strike aircraft would never have to meet modern land-based fighters, was long discredited, and the FAA needed a faster, more heavily armed machine for that role.

In truth, the process of phasing the Swordfish out in the TSR role had gone on far longer than the Admiralty had anticipated when it first elected to continue the type in production in favour of more Albacores. The Barracuda only began to arrive in September 1942, some 18 months later than expected back in 1939 due to decisions made by the Ministry of Aircraft Production in 1940 and organisational dysfunction at Fairey. Where Swordfish could be replaced with Albacores, they had been, but generally there were only enough of the newer aircraft to maintain the new squadrons that had been formed in 1940/1. Deliveries of that type ended in December 1942, meaning it was on borrowed time and squadrons could be maintained only as long as existing stocks held out.

Even more seriously, from the end of 1941, the Royal Navy found itself fighting on a new front, against a new enemy.

9

NEW FRONTS

UNTIL DECEMBER 1941, work for Royal Navy carriers in the Indian Ocean chiefly involved hunting for surface raiders. In February and March that year, Swordfish of 814 Squadron operating from HMS *Hermes* had worked with the cruiser *Hawkins* to intercept Axis ships attempting to flee Mogadishu after Indian troops were landed in Somaliland. Eight Italian and two German ships were apprehended thanks to reports from the Swordfish.

The sudden Japanese advance following a surprise declaration of war in December 1941 changed all that, and the Indian Ocean was suddenly a distinctly hot zone of operations. In March 1942, a Japanese fleet under Admiral Nagumo sailed into the Indian Ocean, carrying out raids on Ceylon and attacking Allied warships. On 15 April, 814 Squadron disembarked, and was ashore when *Hermes* was attacked by overwhelming numbers of Japanese dive-bombers and sunk.

The threat posed by a strong Japanese military presence in the Indian Ocean could not be underestimated, as it threatened Britain's links with Australia and India, and even rendered the loss of India a possibility.

The painful lesson from the brush with the Imperial Japanese Navy (IJN) was that the biplane TSRs were not viable in situations when they might meet Japanese carrier fighters. Somerville, now Commander-in-Chief of the Eastern Fleet, informed the Admiralty that rather than "subjecting my slow Albacores and Swordfish to so unequal a contest", he would seek to remain on the defensive if the IJN was detected during daylight, attempting to force the enemy to make a strike at long range in the hope of maximising enemy losses He noted that he was embarking another Fulmar squadron in each of his two carriers, displacing six Swordfish from *Formidable* and six Albacores from *Indomitable*. Their Lordships regarded this as an "unattractive" policy, but there seems little doubt that sending Swordfish and Albacores against the Mitsubishi A6M 'Zero' in daylight, even with Fulmars escorting, would have been sending the crews to their deaths. Somerville was adamant that with the quality of aircraft at his disposal (strike aircraft and fighters) he could not countenance a daylight attack, though acknowledged that the possession of aircraft with ASV gave the RN opportunities at night and in poor weather that the IJN lacked.[45]

At this point, the hitherto ignored island of Madagascar became a factor in RN thinking. Madagascar was governed by the hostile Vichy French regime, and if used as a base for Japanese submarines, could represent a catastrophe for the

A Swordfish rigged as a target tug – note the windmill winch for winding the target in – flies low over the deck of HMS *Indomitable* ready to cut the wire and deposit the drogue on deck, after a session of gunnery training in the spring of 1942. By this time, the Swordfish was becoming superseded in its original role – *Indomitable*'s strike squadrons were never equipped with Swordfish.

Allies. Plans were therefore drawn up to seize the island.

HMS *Illustrious*, after her severe damage in the Mediterranean, had been repaired and given upgrades to weaponry and aircraft handling and by the beginning of 1942 was back in the UK (although she needed further repairs after a collision with *Formidable* en route) and ready to embark squadrons. Many of the aircrews were inexperienced. Commander 'Bertie' Vigrass, then a junior officer, was one of the new pilots who would first see action during this operation:

> I joined my first operational squadron directly from my advanced pilot training course in January 1942. The squadron was No. 829 Squadron flying Swordfish aircraft. We embarked in HMS *Illustrious* at the beginning of March when I carried out my first deck landing. The ship sailed south from the Clyde and around the Cape of Good Hope to Durban and then to the northern tip of Madagascar where we took part in Operation *Ironclad* – the invasion of Madagascar. This was where I dropped my first torpedo, bombs and depth charges against an enemy.[46]

Illustrious and *Indomitable* were assigned to the invasion force, while *Formidable* would sail with the Eastern Fleet, patrolling in the Indian Ocean against the possibility of the Japanese Navy intervening. During her voyage south, *Illustrious* lost 12 Swordfish, one lost on operations and 11 destroyed in a hangar fire. Replacement aircraft were obtained from Freetown. These Swordfish were then fitted with ASV, beacon receivers and IFF (Identification Friend/Foe) at sea.

The invasion force arrived off the northern tip of the island on 4 May, and shortly before the following dawn, *Illustrious* flew off a striking force of 18 Swordfish in three flights, some armed with bombs and others with torpedoes, to neutralise French warships in Diego Suarez Bay. The French were caught completely unawares, and the Swordfish sank the auxiliary cruiser *Bougainville* with torpedoes and bombed the submarine *Bévéziers* before they had a chance to escape the harbour. *Bévéziers'* commander quickly attempted to weigh anchor, without a third of her crew, but the boat came under accurate dive-bombing from the Swordfish. One bomb blew the submarine's anti-aircraft machine gun off its mountings, ending any chance of defending itself, and other bombs finished the vessel off. The surviving crew made it ashore and participated in the defence against the Allied troops that had landed to take the port.

The sloop *D'Entrecasteaux*, however, evaded the torpedoes launched at her. She was designed as a colonial gunboat, and her draught was so shallow the torpedoes passed harmlessly beneath her hull, though she was set on fire by Sea Hurricanes strafing. She managed to escape to the north, continuing to bombard the commandos ashore through the day with her three 5.4in guns. It was a temporary respite only, as the following day, four Swordfish attacked her again with bombs, scoring multiple hits including a direct hit to the bridge area; the attacks were pressed home despite the small ship's relatively heavy AA armament of 37mm cannon. She sank in shallow water, with only the battered superstructure remaining above the surface, and was abandoned. The submarine *Héros* also escaped destruction on the first day, but a Swordfish from *Illustrious* flown by Sub-Lieutenant Alexander caught up with her on the 7th, and sank her to the north-west of Diego Suarez with depth charges.

Within two days of the first assault, any threat posed to the invasion by naval forces had been neutralised, largely through the actions of *Illustrious'* Swordfish. The two carriers had flown 309 sorties for the loss of four aircraft. It was to be the last time Swordfish would operate in its designed role from a fleet carrier, though the aircraft would persist in the anti-shipping role from land bases for some time to come.

The invasion successfully initiated, in June *Illustrious* joined the Eastern Fleet for a major fleet exercise in the Indian Ocean, patrols, and an offensive sweep off Burma as a diversion from the US Navy's Guadalcanal campaign. The squadrons were re-organised with 829 merging into 810 Squadron to form a double-strength unit, increasingly common in the FAA during that period. In September, she returned to Madagascar to support the final operations in the occupation, and remained with the Eastern Fleet for the rest of the year when, as Bertie Vigrass recounted, everything changed:

> In January 1943 HMS *Illustrious* received a dramatic recall to the Home Fleet. I think that this was because the aircraft carrier *Indomitable* had been taken out of service after having been damaged when in the Mediterranean by a torpedo dropped from an Italian or German aircraft.*

---

* *Indomitable* was heavily damaged in August 1942 and returned to the UK in February 1943 – however, after her post-refit trials she was taken aside again for installation of new aircraft warning radar sets and fighter direction equipment, so this may have been the reason *Illustrious* was recalled at short notice.

In 1942, HMS *Illustrious*, having completed repairs after the severe damage she sustained in January 1942, operated in the Indian Ocean including the invasion of Madagascar. Here two maintainers in cold-weather clothing inspect a Swordfish propeller from an aircraft of 810 or 829 Squadron during that period.

We sailed from Mombasa to the Clyde at high speed with no escorts — not even a guard ship to cover aircraft accidents during take-off and landing. Aircrew were not at all happy about this situation. However, we were required to carry out anti-submarine searches every day and also fighter aircraft patrols when appropriate. One Swordfish did crash into the sea off the Cape when trying to land on after an anti-submarine patrol. Only outstanding seamanship on the part of the ship's company saved the lives of the three airmen.

With the ship's arrival back in the Clyde in early February [810] Squadron disembarked to Machrihanish to continue operational training. At the beginning of April we received the shock news that the Squadron was to be re-equipped with Barracuda aircraft. We were given six weeks in which to learn to fly the aircraft and to work up before re-embarkation.

It is remarkable in many ways that an aircraft that had been in line to go out of production in 1939 and out of service in 1940 had remained in its intended frontline role until April 1943. The previous month, 830 Squadron had finally been disbanded, though for some time it had only existed on paper and its few remaining Swordfish supplemented the aircraft of 828 NAS. Those two squadrons between them were believed to have sunk 30 Axis ships and damaged a further fifty. Nevertheless, the qualities of the Swordfish meant that it was far from ready to retire.

In 1941, Allied and Axis forces grappled over the Atlantic convoys, the vital stream of supplies without which Britain could not survive. As the year progressed, the chief risk swung between long-range maritime patrol bombers and U-boats. Some success in developing surface escorts, with more vessels, better weapons and improved detection technology had helped but was countered by an ever-increasing number of Axis submarines. Long-range aircraft operating from the UK, Canada and later Iceland, could cover most of the area but a 300-mile gap remained where no air reconnaissance was possible.

Without full coverage of the convoy routes, U-boats could simply concentrate in the areas anti-submarine aircraft could not reach. The so-called 'Atlantic Gap' became of paramount importance.

In later 1940, the Admiralty had begun to consider ways in which aircraft might accompany convoys. These included fitting out merchantmen to launch aircraft by catapult or with rocket assistance, and even a scheme to fit a full-length flight deck to a merchant ship hull to create a mini-aircraft carrier.[47] After initial scepticism about the latter idea was overcome, matters progressed extremely quickly and work on the first auxiliary

Personnel of No. 1 Naval Air Gunners' School (NAGS), Yarmouth, Nova Scotia, in 1943, posing with one of the school's 43 Swordfish Mk IIs. This establishment was set up under the British Commonwealth Air Training Plan to train Fleet Air Arm gunners jointly between the Royal Navy and the Royal Canadian Air Force (RCAF).

carrier, *Audacity*, began on 21 January, just six weeks after the idea was discussed by the Naval Air Department.

The initial focus was on fighter aircraft to defend against the feared Focke-Wulf Fw 200 Condor patrol bombers, but as 1941 progressed, the focus shifted to anti-submarine warfare; on 6 December, the First Lord of the Admiralty remarked, "at present the idea of using these Carriers for anti-submarine purposes is predominant."[48] Indeed, just days beforehand, Treasury approval had been granted for an order of 400 more Swordfish to equip the new carriers.

Swordfish were not necessarily the first choice for this role. Earlier that year, in July, 811 Squadron had been equipped with the Vought Chesapeake, as the Royal Navy termed the SB2U Vindicator scout-bomber. That month, HMS *Audacity*, the first of the escort carriers, began its deck-landing trials. However, *Audacity* was at that time focused on air defence, and in its short career would only operate fighters. By November, 811 Squadron's Chesapeakes had proven unsuitable. The type required too great a take-off run for the short escort carrier flight decks, so they were replaced with Swordfish in November, the very month the order for 400 Swordfish for escort carriers was confirmed. Of course, the Swordfish had operated in the anti-submarine role from fleet carriers since the beginning of the war, with some success.

The Swordfish from the December 1941 order would be the Mk II, a modestly upgraded version of

Three air-to-air photographs of NAGS Swordfish above the Nova Scotia landscape. The two nearest aircraft, HS320 'L' and HS263, were formally taken on charge by the RCAF in January/February 1943, though they still wore Royal Navy colours and insignia.

the Mk I, which had served the Fleet Air Arm from the type's introduction in 1935 to date. The first Mk II would roll off the Sherburn production line, appropriately enough, in December 1941, the same month as convoy HG76 departed from Gibraltar. In truth it was very little different from the Mk I – the chief distinction was an upgraded engine, a Pegasus 30 (and even this becomes confused, as Mk Is were frequently re-engined with the more powerful unit). The main visual difference between Swordfish Mk I and Mk II was the larger oil cooler (visible on the port side of the nose behind the engine) required by the latter's more powerful and tropical-rated engine, with a distinctive removable blanking plate to prevent over-cooling when not operating in tropical climates.*

Somewhat ironically in view of the First Sea Lord's opinion that the anti-submarine role had become 'predominant' for escort carriers, *Audacity* never carried Swordfish operationally. Her Martlet fighters were expected to operate in that role as well as dealing with shadowing aircraft, despite having nothing but their 5in machine guns to attack with. Even more surprisingly, when *Audacity* was waiting at Gibraltar in December 1941 for convoy HG76 to depart, the chance to embark some Swordfish was passed up, even though the carrier had only four Martlets on board. After the loss of *Ark Royal*, 812 Squadron remained at North Front with the carrier's surviving Swordfish. According to RN historian Kenneth Poolman,

> The Admiralty suggested to the C-in-C, Western Approaches, and the Flag Officer Commanding North Atlantic that *Audacity* should embark two or three of the Swordfish now at Gibraltar to improve the anti-submarine capacity of the convoy escorts. But the idea was not taken up, the reasons given being a shortage of observers and telegraphist-air-gunners as well as a lack of R/T sets to put in the aircraft.[49]

The Kriegsmarine employed 'wolfpack' tactics for convoy hunting, with groups of U-boats coordinating their attacks rather than individual boats attacking separately as had been more common at the beginning of the war. The Straits of Gibraltar being a 'chokepoint' for Allied convoys in and out of the Mediterranean, it was a natural place for U-boats to assemble. Indeed, the departure of the convoy had been postponed because of indications of large numbers of U-boats in the vicinity. Even though 812 Squadron's Swordfish would not be embarked on *Audacity*, they would support the convoy for as long as it was in range.

The convoy sailed on 14 December in the afternoon. At 2325 that night, six and a half miles off the convoy's starboard beam, 812 Squadron Swordfish 'X' detected a contact on ASV some three and a half miles away, which closer inspection revealed to be a U-boat approaching the convoy. The Swordfish flew in from astern and dropped three depth charges – two fell ahead of the submarine, the third to starboard. Unfortunately, with no R/T set, the Swordfish could not inform the convoy or direct the escort towards the contact, but the attack had at least dissuaded the submarine from its attack. At 0135, aircraft 'X' sighted another U-boat 10 miles astern of the convoy and dived at it as if to make an attack, though it had dropped all its depth charges while attacking the first U-boat. The submarine quickly submerged. Later in the morning, at 0537, Swordfish 'B' located a U-boat off Cape Trafalgar and dropped two depth charges directly on the spot where it had just 'crash dived', but saw no evidence of damage.

It was unfortunate that lack of equipment prevented the embarkation of some Swordfish

---

* Many published sources state that the distinguishing feature of the Swordfish Mk II was metal-skinned lower mainplane undersides, but this feature was not required until 1943 when rocket projectiles began to be carried. The first Mk IIs were delivered in late 1941.

on *Audacity*, as the carrier was torpedoed and sunk by a U-boat on the way back to the UK. As it turned out, though, the ASV-equipped Swordfish proved the ideal mount for patrolling the straits at night. At this time, as well as trying to ambush convoys outside Gibraltar, an increasing number of U-boats were attempting to pass through the straits and into the Mediterranean. Many tried to sneak through on the surface at night, and between 30 November and 21 December 1941, 812 Squadron flew 300 hours for this purpose.

On the night of 21 December, one 812 aircraft spotted the U-boat *U-451*, commanded by Korvettenkapitän E. Hoffmann, north-west of Tangier, about to enter the narrows. The Swordfish attacked with depth charges and sank the U-boat, this being the first submarine to be destroyed by an aircraft at night. No U-boats attempted to make the crossing until the following spring, so successful were the countermeasures of which 812 Squadron was now a part.

In any event, the lessons of HG76 had been learned, and the next escort carriers to commission would have Swordfish in its air group. While further British conversions like *Audacity* were planned, they were competing with many other priorities for shipyard capacity, so the first escort carriers to follow the pioneer were US-built vessels then known as BAVGs, but which would later be designated by the more familiar title of CVE.*

This was fortuitous, as when the British approached the US to ask if they could build more carriers like *Audacity*, the Americans had already begun their own programme, the first such ship being USS *Long Island*, commissioned in June 1941. The first of the 'BAVGs' to commission was HMS *Archer* in November 1941, followed by *Avenger* in March 1942. In fact, when *Audacity* was sunk, *Archer* was already on her trials, but due to numerous reliability problems, particularly with her engines, and a collision, it took time before she was ready for operational service.

In the meantime, the Admiralty and other senior RN figures reinforced that Swordfish was the most suitable aircraft available for the escort carrier role, with strengths that more modern types could not match. The commanding officer of 812 Squadron, Lieutenant-Commander G. Woods, wrote of "the superiority of the Swordfish aircraft for night A/S patrols and attacks in comparison with any other types of modern aircraft", highlighting "its comparatively low speed, manoeuvrability and open cockpit [which] gives better opportunities for sighting, holding contact and making an immediate attack", while experience showed that the positioning of the ASV aerials on the Swordfish was more suitable than would be possible on a monoplane and made it "easier to hold a contact on the screen, as the range closes, without losing too much in the sea echo". Woods concluded that "Owing to being quieter, smaller and therefore less visible, the Swordfish has a greater chance of achieving a surprise attack."[50]

The Director of Naval Air Division concurred, noting that the Swordfish "appears to be the most suitable TSR for auxiliary carriers", and "the foregoing shows in DNAD's opinion, the great advantage to be gained by perpetuating the Swordfish".[51] British thinking was coloured at this time by the erroneous belief that monoplane TSRs** such as the Barracuda and Avenger would be too large and heavy to operate from escort carriers. In fact,

---

* US Navy escort carriers initially had the abbreviation 'AVG' referring to Auxiliary Aircraft Escort Vessel, and those assigned to the Royal Navy received the prefix 'B'. The abbreviation for escort carriers would change to ACV (Auxiliary Carrier Vessel), then CVE (Carrier Vessel, Escort). By early 1943, the UK term 'auxiliary carrier' had changed to 'escort carrier', and it was in this manner that they would chiefly be known from then on, although the British used them extensively for other purposes as well.

** At around this time the designation was changing from Torpedo-Spotter-Reconnaissance, or TSR, to Torpedo-Bomber-Reconnaissance, or TBR, but the former term is used here for simplicity

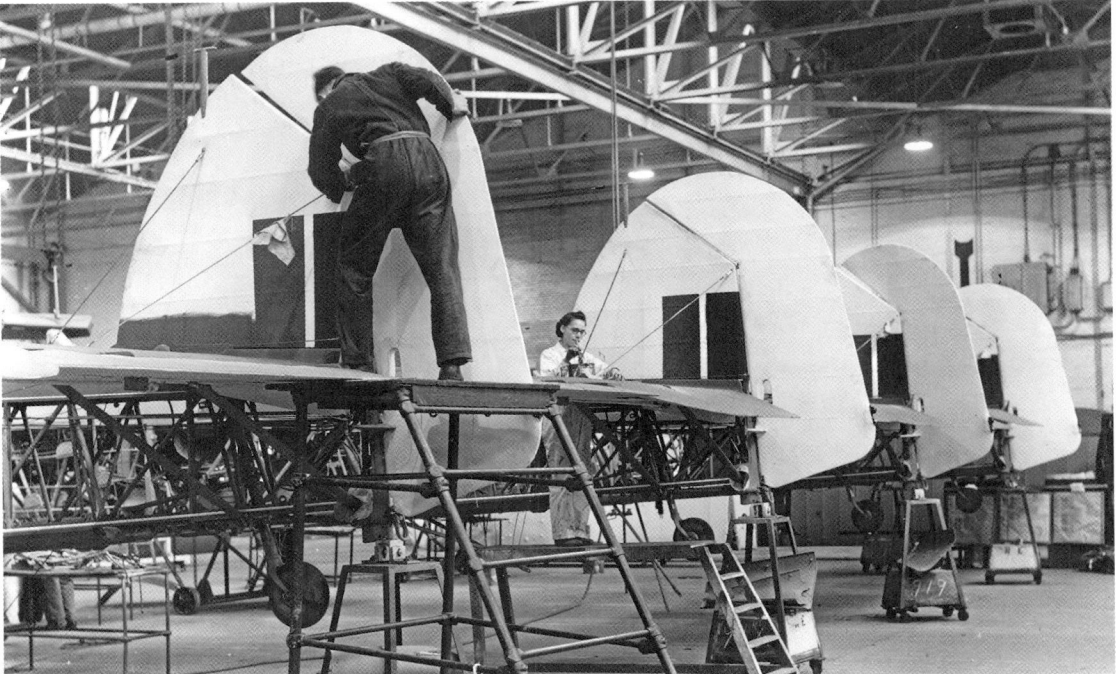

The Swordfish production line at Sherburn producing aircraft known colloquially as 'Blackfish'. This factory completed 1,701 Swordfish between 1940 and 1944, considerably more than the parent company ever built.

both types would be able to operate successfully from small decks when catapults or rocket-assist were used. It was clear that the Admiralty was also overestimating the advantages of Swordfish, such as slow speed for loitering, during this phase, and underestimating the disadvantages such as lack of performance, load-carrying ability and relatively weak undercarriage. Although both of these attitudes would change within months, during this period the Fleet Air Arm's requirements for aircraft were largely set in stone with the result that the Swordfish soldiered on rather longer than was ideal.

As things stood, the Swordfish, along with the Albacore, was intended to be phased out of production by the middle of 1943. The desire for aircraft for escort carriers, and the presumed superiority of the Swordfish, however, meant that by April 1942, orders for the type rose to 650, with the Admiralty asking for Treasury approval to boost numbers on order to 1,000, which would keep Blackburn's Sherburn-in-Elmet factory occupied until mid-1944.

At this time, the development of 'cordite impulse assisted take-off gear' (later known as rocket-assisted take-off Gear, or RATOG) was requested to enable aircraft to be launched at heavier all-up weights. The Fifth Sea Lord said that this "should be pressed on with as an urgent requirement for auxiliary carriers" at a meeting with Air Ministry representatives on 3 April 1942.[52] This would not be available for some time, however and was not in widespread use by Swordfish until two years later.

The first of the US-supplied escort carriers, HMS *Archer*, was intended from the start to carry both Swordfish and fighters, unlike *Audacity*, and in fact the first of her two squadrons to embark was 834 NAS with its Swordfish Mk Is in March 1942, in time for *Archer*'s shakedown cruise to West African waters. Unfortunately, this voyage was plagued with reliability problems, though 834 NAS was able to put in many hours' flying; in the often-calm waters to be found around Freetown, the aircrews found how challenging it was to fly off a Swordfish heavy with fuel and depth charges from such a short deck. The maiden cruise of HMS *Archer* was less than auspicious. She had been meant to join a convoy escort from Freetown, but the ongoing problems with her machinery precluded it. Two Swordfish were heavily damaged in landing accidents early on. Another was damaged by 'friendly fire' when trying to drop a message to US forces on Ascension Island about a raider in the area. One more Swordfish went over the side causing the death of the TAG, while a bomb exploded when armourers were handling it, killing nine men and damaging the hangar and a Swordfish. At one point, the engines broke down completely with 26 U-boats in the area. Finally, an outbreak of flu laid all the aircrew low, leaving the Commander Flying the only fit qualified pilot. *Archer* limped back to the US for repairs and a refit in July 1942.

10

BATTLING THE WOLFPACKS

AVENGER SAILED from the US with convoy AT15 at the end of April 1942, picking up the Swordfish of 816 Squadron from Palisadoes, Jamaica, on 3 May to provide anti-submarine protection, this squadron having reformed there after the loss of *Ark Royal*. *Biter* followed a couple of weeks later, also picking up a Swordfish squadron — 836 NAS — from Palisadoes for the passage.

The experience on Arctic convoys had reinforced the need for fighter protection first and foremost, due to the convoy route being in range of aircraft from Norway. Besides, the need for anti-submarine aircraft was still acute, and 825 Squadron, rebuilding after the losses during the Channel Dash, was assigned to *Avenger*'s air group with three Swordfish Mk IIs and five crews.

The conditions on convoy PQ18 to Murmansk were not favourable, both in terms of enemy action — the convoy came under repeated, heavy air attack — and weather. The first anti-submarine patrol flown, on 10 September, was met with worsening conditions and finally snow driving into the Swordfish's open cockpits. The Swordfish made it back to *Avenger* but was damaged during the landing. The Swordfish crews' jobs were not made any easier by restrictions on the use of R/T imposed to prevent German direction-finding equipment from locating the convoy. Early in the voyage, several U-boats were spotted but could not be reported until the Swordfish had returned to *Avenger*, giving the surface escorts little chance to engage them. Fortunately, radio silence was relaxed after a couple of days. In the early morning of 14 September, Sub-Lieutenant Evans sighted and attacked a U-boat, then attempted to dogfight with a lurking Heinkel He 111, but the shadower stayed clear. Later that morning, Evans spotted a U-boat south of Spitzbergen and dropped a depth charge on it, then called up the escorts to finish the job. HMS *Onslow* arrived and sank the damaged submarine, which turned out to be *U-589*. The credit for the sinking was shared between the destroyer and 825 Squadron.

The Sea Hurricanes of 802 and 882 Squadrons were busiest of *Avenger*'s aircraft on PQ18, but 825 Squadron still had plenty to do. By 16 September, the convoy was within range of shore-based aircraft from Russia, and the Swordfish could be packed away so as not to hamper the operations of the fighters. When PQ18 arrived, 21 of the original 31 ships had survived the passage, three of the 10 lost to U-boats. It was far from perfect but was an improvement on previous convoys.

Nevertheless, the verdict of RN historian Kenneth Poolman — who himself served as an RN officer on convoy service — on the Swordfish for

Fine air-to-air study of Blackburn-built Swordfish Mk I V4719 'K' of 835 Squadron in April–June 1942. This squadron formed in Palisadoes, Jamaica, in February, this being one of its original aircraft, before returning to the UK in April. Its Mk I Swordfish were never used operationally, the squadron changing to Mk IIs before embarking in its first carrier, the escort vessel *Battler*.

convoy work was little short of scathing, describing them as "pitifully inadequate".[53] Commander Colthurst, *Avenger*'s captain, was marginally more measured:

> The operation of Swordfish on anti-submarine patrols and for other work from auxiliary aircraft carriers is not satisfactory. Their take-off when heavily loaded is inadequate for a 440ft flight deck with a maximum speed of 16 knots and normal strengths of wind. There will be few occasions when a Swordfish force of any size can be flown off with torpedoes or a full load of depth charges.[54]

The third carrier from the US was HMS *Biter*, which was handed over to the RN at Brooklyn in May 1942 and took on her first aircraft — a Swordfish — on 2 June. Ten days later she set off across the Atlantic, despite the seemingly inevitable engine trouble that affected most of the early US-built auxiliary carriers. Five days after her departure, disaster was narrowly averted when one of her Swordfish crashed into the carrier's island while carrying a depth charge. Fortunately, it did not go off, and after a tense extraction, was disposed of safely. By the end of the month, she was in dock at Greenock undergoing modification to British standards. Afterwards, the opportunity was taken to carry out deck-landing trials of various Fleet Air Arm types. While these were taking place, *Biter* was joined at Greenock by *Dasher*, the last of the US-built escort carriers to be powered by the troublesome diesel engines. Subsequent vessels (from *Attacker* onwards) would be steam turbine

HMS *Avenger* was the second US-built escort carrier in RN service, and is best known for her sterling performance during convoy PQ18, as seen here. *Avenger*'s contribution is chiefly remembered for the Sea Hurricanes of 802 Squadron, but the Swordfish of 825 Squadron maintained constant anti-submarine patrols during daylight, in highly challenging conditions, and claimed one submarine sunk with surface escorts.

powered. Joining the US-built escort carriers in September 1942 was the second of the British-built vessels, HMS *Activity*, which was diesel powered like the early US vessels, but around 80 feet longer.

By the early autumn of 1942, *Avenger* and *Biter* were in the UK preparing to escort convoys. A new type of auxiliary carrier was also on its way. Earlier in the year, the Admiralty had accepted the idea of a hybrid carrier that essentially consisted of a flight deck attached to a functioning merchant ship, which would continue to operate under the Red Ensign and be crewed by civilian sailors, but carry a small number of Swordfish for anti-submarine protection. The two types of merchant ship chosen were bulk grain carriers and heavy oil tankers, as they were loaded by hose and did not require large hatches in the deck to access the hold. In October 1942, the First Lord of the Admiralty informed Churchill that "We are pressing on with the supply of these ships in conjunction with the Ministry of War Transport."[55]

Biter and *Avenger* were mainly equipped with fighters for their forthcoming voyages, but both had small Swordfish detachments from 833 Squadron. In fact, their next operation would not be one of the usual convoys but the invasion of French North Africa, Operation *Torch*. To ensure the transfer of the vast invasion fleet had as much cover as possible, Russian and Gibraltar convoys were suspended. The handful of Swordfish that took part in the North African landings were used for anti-submarine patrols, while Albacores represented the FAA in the strike role.

The operation was no less risky than convoy escorts. *Avenger* had concluded her role with the landings, and was proceeding home as part of the escort for a convoy of vessels that had taken part in Operation *Torch* but were now no longer required off the beachhead. While off the Portuguese coast in the early morning of 15 November, U-boats were detected. Two transports were torpedoed, and then a third torpedo struck *Avenger* on the port side, near her bomb room. According to the subsequent inquiry, the room "Contained 500lb and 250lb SAP bombs, 40lb GP bombs, depth charges and smoke floats". Witnesses aboard the *Ulster Monarch* described "A vivid red flash on the starboard side of *Avenger* stretching the whole length of the ship." The carrier "Disappeared entirely within three minutes of the explosion. It may have been even less than two minutes".[56] There were only 12 survivors – 514 men lost their lives. No Swordfish crews were aboard, as the detachment of 833 Squadron had disembarked to Gibraltar a couple of weeks previously, but the loss brought it home to aircrews operating from 'Woolworth carriers' how low their chances of survival were in the event of a torpedo hit or comparable catastrophe. The loss of *Avenger* would be followed a few months later by the total loss of another US-built escort carrier.

Indeed, while escort carriers from the US were a godsend for the UK, they were not considered entirely suitable as delivered. In February 1943, the Admiralty met to consider the use of escort carriers in the immediate future, and necessary

Royal Navy Fairey Swordfish LS422 bounced into the barrier of HMS *Battler* on 1 September 1945. This aircraft had originally equipped 744 Squadron, the training unit for merchant aircraft carrier (MAC) ships, before transferring to 768 squadron, a deck-landing training unit.

modifications to enable them to meet the RN's needs. The latter included lengthening the flight deck and fitting further bulkheads to the bomb rooms which had proved so disastrous to *Avenger* in their original state sitting directly against the ship's side.[57] The carriers were deemed unsuitable for the fast 'CU' series of transatlantic convoys,* as they had insufficient margin of speed, but would be used for protection of North Atlantic trade routes. Russian convoys would each have two escort carriers, with *Dasher* and *Battler* earmarked for the next one. *Activity*, the second British-built carrier, was to be reserved for deck-landing training, while *Archer*, being less suitable for the Russian run due to being able to carry fewer fighters, was to be used on North Atlantic convoys. Many more ships were coming through, including the first five of the larger, faster US-built Attacker-class carriers. These were to be accepted "with the minimum of modifications for Trade protection" — although events would soon revise that view.

By the time convoys were ready to resume following the disruption caused by the North African landings, the winter weather made air cover both less practicable and less important. This was particularly so for the Arctic convoys. However, the weather would soon improve and the new escort carriers would have to be ready.

To mark this new phase of the Swordfish's war, it would gain a distinctive new appearance. White camouflage on undersides and sides was adopted in late 1942 for aircraft flying from escort carriers as it was deemed the most effective colour for flying over the sea during daytime.

---

* Tankers sailing directly from petroleum refineries at Curaçao to the United Kingdom.

Mk II HS158 demonstrating the rocket rails now fitted as standard equipment from the factory (with a metal skin on the wing underside to protect the fabric from sparks). This aircraft went first to 813 Squadron in North Africa in December 1942, before going to 860 Squadron, the unit supplying Swordfish and crews to the two Dutch MAC ships.

The US-built escort carrier *Dasher* was hurriedly prepared to begin its operational career in February 1943, with Swordfish provided by 816 Squadron which had been operating with RAF Coastal Command over the English Channel since May 1942. *Dasher* experienced a false start when bad weather caused cracks to open up in her hull as she was en route to join convoy JW53. She returned to the UK for repairs ahead of the time when improving weather would make protection from both U-boats and enemy aircraft vital.

At the end of March, 816 squadron was taking advantage of the delay to work up properly with the new carrier and its counterpart Sea Hurricane squadron when *Dasher* blew up and sank in the Clyde. The most likely explanation was that this was due to an aviation fuel explosion triggered by an open flame igniting vapour from the notoriously leaky petrol system. The board of inquiry concluded that it was probably a cigarette or possibly a short in the lighting that sparked the fatal explosion, but the secrecy that followed the sinking led alternative theories to spring up, one of which involved the ship's Swordfish. Indeed, the carrier had been operating aircraft shortly before the explosion and according to the board of inquiry, one of the Swordfish had just landed, while the other two were being fuelled.

George Humphreys, a seaman on the landing craft *LCT 523* taking part in an exercise in the Kyles of Bute, happened to be observing *Dasher* at the time of the explosion. He recalled:

> I pointed the telescope down the Kyles of Bute towards the entrance of the Clyde, and sure enough, an aircraft carrier and its stern facing up the Kyles of Bute was visible ... a plane was coming along its port side to land aboard the aircraft carrier ... I'm watching it, and the plane instead of the flight deck, went straight into the quarterdeck and caught fire, see?[58]

LCT 523 immediately moved to render assistance, but seeing boats coming out of Ardrossan, turned back and the crew did not see what happened afterwards. The board of inquiry made no mention of a Swordfish crash being the cause of the fire, and it seems most likely that Humphreys, at great distance and having little experience of aircraft carriers, misinterpreted what he saw.* Nevertheless, questions around the sinking remain to this day, and the event had just as severe an effect on the communities that were home to many of the sailors as it did on the Fleet Air Arm. This was felt most acutely in 819 Squadron, which lost all of the rating maintainers who were in the hangar at the time of the explosion, likely killed instantly.

More widely, the sinking had the effect of delaying the widespread use of escort carriers still further, while the potentially dangerous aviation fuel systems on the lend-lease carriers were reworked to safer British standards.

The early US-supplied carriers were powered by diesel engines which never shook their reputation for unreliability. Peter Jinks, a Swordfish TAG with 819 Squadron, which joined HMS *Archer* in early 1943, recalled the difficulties:

> We were on what they called 'Woolworth carriers' or 'Banana Boats', the first ones converted in the USA from actual merchant ships. They were merchant ships actually that carried bananas, they belonged to a company that ran the fruit cargo ships in the Pacific to San Francisco. And they took, I think there were four or five of them, they belonged to a company called the Moore-McCormack Line and they were all well used, and the engines were in pretty poor condition. My first

---

* The author is indebted to Nick Hewitt, curator of the National Museum of the Royal Navy, for making him aware of Humphreys' IWM recordings.

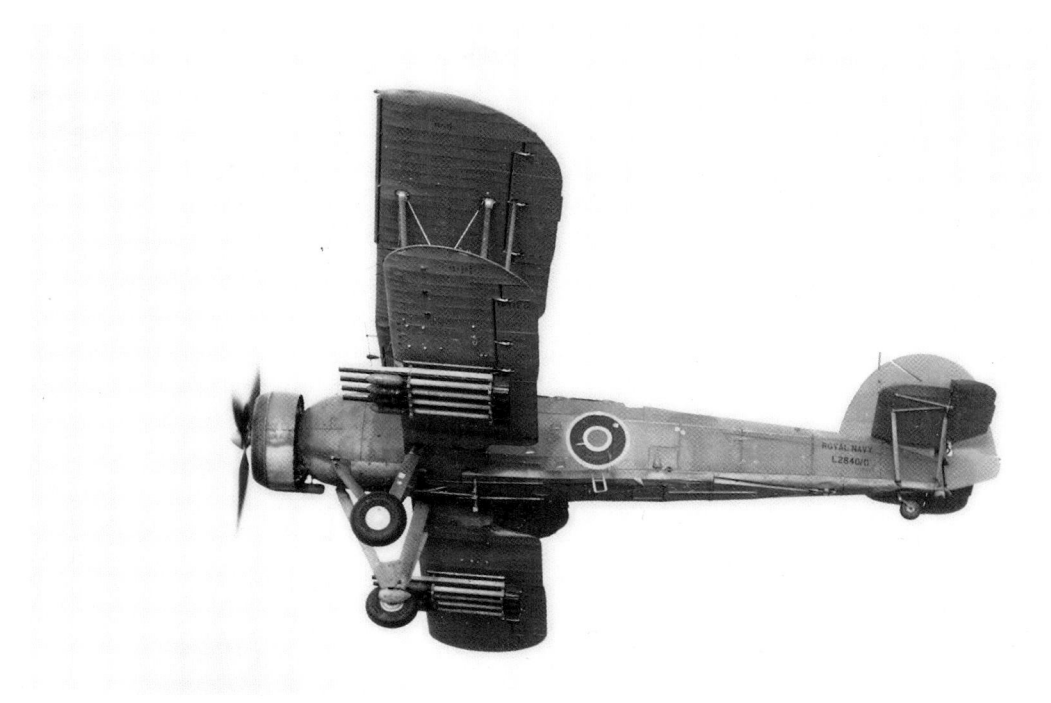

Swordfish Mk I L2840/G at the Aeroplane and Armament Experimental Establishment, Boscombe Down, May/June 1943 where it trialled rocket projectile armament. The G suffix indicates that the aircraft is to be kept under guard at all times.

one was *Archer*, HMS *Archer*. And we were constantly having engine breakdowns at sea.

Even if the engines were running, they often failed to produce full power and a loaded Swordfish would need every inch of *Archer*'s 410-feet flight deck to get airborne. And then only barely. "If the engines weren't pumping well," Peter Jinks said, "you could often feel your wheels go over the bow end of the flight deck, and you'd sort of go down and ... Being in the back seat here, I had a good view of the deck disappearing, and in fact I've seen our slipstream make waves on the water — that low — 'til you climb."[59]

In 1943, the transition of the Swordfish from fleet torpedo bomber to convoy escort specialist was completed. The last use of the aircraft in its designed role had taken place with the Madagascar operations, and although it would operate with the fleet on occasion thereafter, it would overwhelmingly be from escort carriers in the anti-submarine role. The loss of *Dasher* and the resulting delays to newer carriers notwithstanding, the first half of 1943 would prove highly successful for the concept of the escort carriers and the Swordfish that were, for the moment, their main weapon.

It was not a moment too soon. With weather improving from February 1943, large numbers of U-boats were active in the Atlantic once again. In January, 37 ships were sunk, representing just over 200,000 tons. In March, that rose to 108 ships and over 600,000 tons.

Archer and *Biter* had gone into dock for modifications, which were completed by February

Mk II HS275 'J' at 745 training squadron, Yarmouth, Canada, between May 1943 and January 1944. This aircraft was distinguished by nose art depicting the character J. Wellington Wimpy from the 'Popeye' cartoons.

and they took part in joint exercises later in the month. *Archer* carried the traditional two squadrons, one of TSRs and one of fighters, with 819 Squadron providing nine Swordfish supplemented by three Martlets of 892 Squadron. *Biter*, meanwhile, adopted a new arrangement of a single heterogeneous unit, with both Sea Hurricanes and Swordfish belonging to 811 Squadron. This promised advantages for integrating the aircrew on the small carrier, simplifying organisation, and perhaps most importantly, promoting close working and joint tactics between the two types of aircraft. *Biter* would also pioneer a new approach to convoy protection, acting with her destroyer escort as an independent unit giving distant cover to the convoy, a prototype of the later hunter-killer group. *Archer*, meanwhile, was not leaving all the innovation to her counterpart. Her Swordfish would be the first to be equipped with rocket projectiles. After the approval of this weapon for use by Swordfish, following successful trials at the A&AEE in early 1943, the type was modified with part of the lower wing skinned in metal to avoid the efflux setting fire to the fabric.

Biter was first of the pair to become operational, covering convoy ONS4 to Newfoundland from 21 April. Four days later, one of her Swordfish sighted *U-203* and attacked it with depth charges, then marked the spot for a destroyer, which delivered the coup de grâce after a lengthy fight. The rest of the voyage was quiet and the convoy arrived unscathed.

On 3 May, *Archer* sailed from Iceland to join ONS6, and made contact six days later. Despite high winds, the carrier flew off patrols and a Swordfish and its pilot, Sub-Lieutenant Martin, were lost when the aircraft crashed over the side. The carrier reached Canada on the 16th without having yet engaged a U-boat.

Swordfish Mk II HS533 training aircrews in Canada. This aircraft was one of a number to be retrofitted with a Fairey-designed and locally produced glazed cockpit canopy to improve crew comfort in cold weather. The canopy was only used on training aircraft (bestowing the unofficial designation Mk IV) despite the conditions on the North Atlantic and Russian convoys which would have made an enclosed cockpit welcome.

Meanwhile, on 5 May, *Biter* began the return journey from Newfoundland, covering convoy HX237, again in a 'semi-detached' fashion until the senior officer ordered the carrier to join the convoy proper four days later. One of *Biter*'s Swordfish joined an attack on a U-boat on 10 May, and the crew were unpleasantly surprised to find the submarine remaining stubbornly on the surface, where it was at little risk from their depth charges, and defending themselves trenchantly with their 20mm Flak. *Biter*'s Swordfish took hits and was replaced on scene by another aircraft, but the second machine got lost and could not find the carrier, eventually ditching by a merchantman.

The next day, several U-boats were detected via the radio transmissions used by the wolfpacks to coordinate their attacks, and despite worsening weather, the carrier flew off patrols. A Swordfish located one and depth-charged it, but again, it remained on the surface, trying to keep the aircraft at bay with its 20mm cannon. Eventually it was driven to submerge and was not detected again.

It was clear that the U-boats had developed a new and dangerous tactic in response to the appearance of carrier-based aircraft. The following day a Swordfish was brought down by a U-boat's guns, and blew up when its own depth charges detonated. *Biter*'s aircrews were ordered to hold off if a U-boat refused to submerge. Its options then were to make a dive-bombing attack with conventional bombs, if carried, call in reinforcements — particularly a Martlet to strafe the gunners — or simply shadow the submarine until escort vessels could come up.

The day the Swordfish was lost, the convoy came under the umbrella of long-range, land-based aircraft but *Biter*'s aircraft continued to patrol, and on the 13th, joined aircraft of Coastal Command

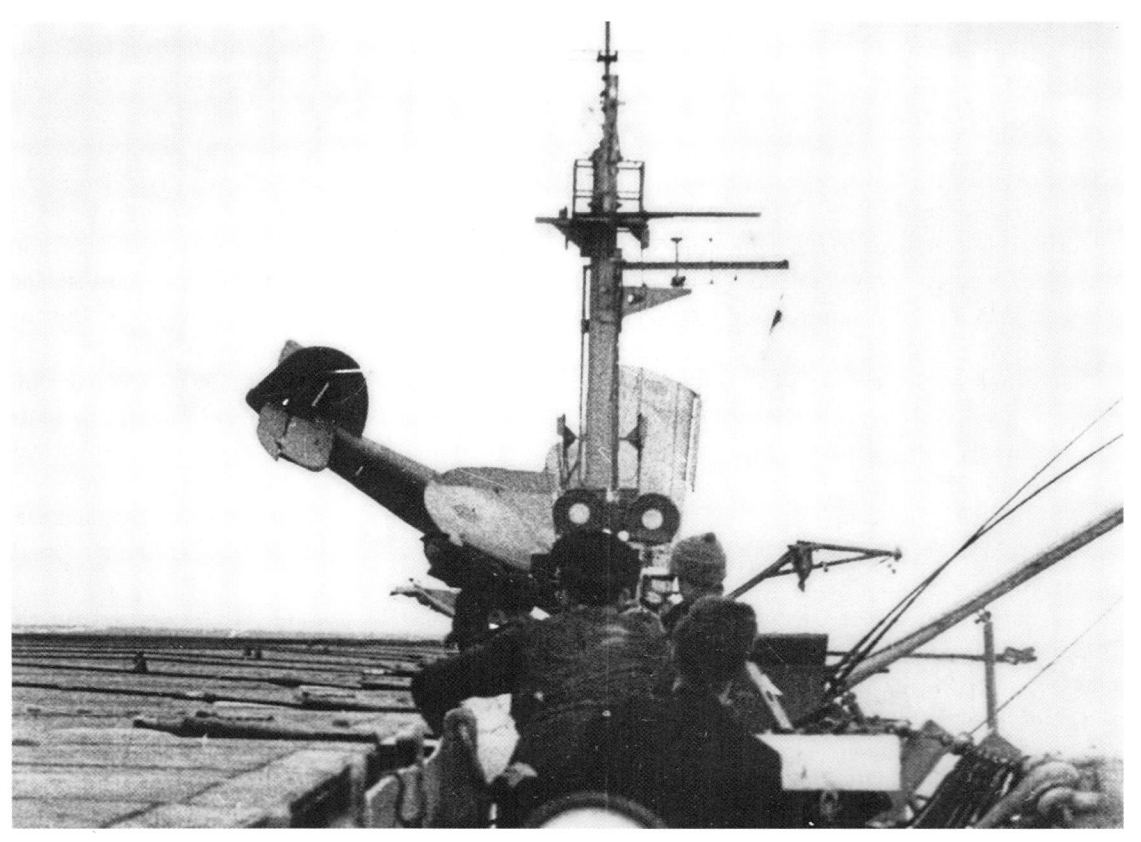

A Swordfish comes to grief on the deck of HMS *Archer*, the first US-built escort carrier in Royal Navy service – 819 Squadron embarked its Swordfish IIs on 28 February 1943, but Sub-Lieutenant Lamb missed the wires in HS362 'G' and floated into the barrier.

and the US Navy in attacking two submarines, which were driven away. *Biter* was then detached to cover another convoy, SC129, and while en route, came across another U-boat. The wind was so light that the only war-load the Swordfish could carry was two 40lb bombs. Nevertheless, the Swordfish attacked – once again, the U-boat remained on the surface – and while the aircraft successfully recovered to the carrier, it had sustained damage. On 16 May, SC129 arrived in the UK without having sustained any losses.

Three days later, *Archer* departed Argentia in Newfoundland to rendezvous with the returning convoy HX239. The convoy was under the protection of land-based aircraft until 22 May, but on that day, U-boat transmissions were detected and a Swordfish from 819 Squadron spotted a submarine on the surface some miles behind the merchantmen. As *Biter*'s aircrews had experienced, the U-boat remained on the surface so *Archer*'s Swordfish wisely called the ship for reinforcements. A second Swordfish and a Martlet were dispatched, and in the ensuing attack, the U-boat was forced to submerge.

This, while no doubt disappointing to the crews, represented a success in itself. In truth, most patrols saw little, and even in cases where attacks took place, actually sinking a submarine without assistance was unlikely. The increasing importance of the Swordfish and the escort carrier was as a deterrent, and a means of preventing the U-boats from reaching an attacking position. TAG Peter Jinks, a veteran of 819 Squadron's spell with HMS *Archer*, said: "Two and a half hour patrols with depth charges keeping the submarines out of the way. The fact that we were there kept them away—they would submerge out of the way. People say 'did you ever see a submarine?' Well, no I didn't! But we never lost a ship from our convoy."

Nevertheless, there were still contacts. The next day, 23 May, Swordfish 'F' spotted a U-boat in a very dangerous position ahead of the convoy. Unusually, it submerged on seeing the Swordfish, but remained at periscope depth allowing the aircraft to track it using the 'feather' where the periscope penetrated the surface. They dropped depth charges, obtaining a perfect 'straddle', inflicting severe damage to the U-boat which caused it to break off and limp back to port. Later that morning, a second U-boat was spotted and attacked without visible results, and a little later still, Swordfish 'B'—which was equipped with rocket projectiles—spotted a third submarine and managed to work into a good position using cloud. Diving out of the cloud, the observer having navigated perfectly, the Swordfish fired off its rockets in salvos of two, getting closer each time until the last pair slammed into the U-boat's hull. The squadron diary remarked, "The submarine sunk by 'B' caught fire aft and suffered severe damage to its steering gear during the Rocket Attack. The crew appeared to be dumbfounded by the new weapon."[60]

Even with their boat crippled and unable to submerge, the crew were not ready to give up and peppered the Swordfish with cannon fire. The Swordfish called up a Martlet, which strafed the conning tower and killed the captain, whereupon the remaining submariners realised the game was up and abandoned ship.

There were no more encounters with U-boats on that trip, though a Swordfish was forced to ditch for mechanical reasons on the 24th. It had been another highly successful trip for one of the still-new carriers and though *Archer* was small and plagued with engine problems, she had protected her convoys magnificently. Her aircraft control was particularly noteworthy, with the fighters and TSRs invariably directed with great precision. Furthermore, cooperation between Swordfish and Martlets had been exemplary, especially allowing for the traditional 'two squadron' structure.

While the Swordfish had shown well, their slow speed made them more vulnerable to U-boats determined to defend themselves with their Flak guns. *Archer*'s Martlets had been so successful that her captain recommended increasing the number of them aboard escort carriers at the expense of some Swordfish.

Ironically, *Biter*'s experience had led her captain to a completely different conclusion. "Martlets did not fly at all," he reported, "and it is considered questionable whether the few occasions on which the conditions would be suitable, justify the valuable space taken up by these aircraft, which would otherwise be used for Swordfish."[61] Later, however, the determined resistance displayed by U-boats under attack caused him to revise his opinion and argue for the retention of Martlets for the support they could provide to Swordfish. The experiences of *Biter* and *Archer* led to a standard procedure for escort carriers where a 'support team' of a fighter and a TSR was held at readiness to respond immediately to a patrol aircraft calling for assistance.

More US-built ships were coming through, and in March 1943, *Hunter* and *Stalker* arrived at Gibraltar after crossing the Atlantic, bound for the Clyde. Here they were detailed to accompany convoy MKF11, although neither carrier had any aircraft or aircrews. The need was such that *Hunter*'s captain was forced to scrape together a complement of machines and crew from the pool at Gibraltar, including four Swordfish and two old Sea Hurricane Mk Is, with two Avenger crews from *Stalker* making up the numbers, and two

A Swordfish Mk II alongside the aircraft that was meant to replace both the Swordfish and Albacore, the Fairey Barracuda. The monoplane is carrying a large mine, while the Swordfish has a load of six 250lb depth charges on its wing carriers.

unserviceable Swordfish due for overhaul service as spares sources. The carrier husbanded these slender resources as best it could, keeping Swordfish patrols to dawn and dusk whenever Coastal Command cover was available, though crashes on deck reduced the complement of Swordfish to two by the morning of 3 April, and the remaining two crashed in the evening. The ship had only a skeleton crew of maintainers, who worked through the night to try to bring one Swordfish to serviceable status. The carrier staggered in to the Clyde on 5 April as a gale was blowing, and to add insult to injury, was unable to anchor securely until late the next day.

That month the first of the new hybrid type of carrier was commissioned. The merchant aircraft carrier, or MAC ship, would remain under civilian command and crew, and would form part of each convoy rather than its escort. They would be purely anti-submarine vessels, without any air-defence capability other than AA guns. *Empire Macalpine*, the first to appear, was a grain carrier, with a small hangar aft and provision for four Swordfish. The first tanker conversion, *Rapana*, would commission in July. The flight decks of these carriers were even smaller than those of the escort carriers, with *Empire Macalpine*'s a mere 414 feet long (though later grain ship-based conversions would have a further 10 feet to play with) and 62 feet wide — 16 feet 6 inches wider than the wingspan of a Swordfish. A special fine-pitch propeller was provided for Swordfish allocated to MAC ships to permit take-off in lighter wind, and for the most part this device was considered essential, though it eroded the already poor performance in the air. "It only did about 80 or 90 miles an hour, a ridiculous speed really," said Brian Ryley, an observer with 836 Squadron on the MAC ship *Empire Macandrew*.[62]

At this time, the Admiralty assessed that it would need 70 additional TSR aircraft a month in 1945. Part of this was to be achieved by increasing Swordfish production by 21% (from 45 to 55 a month) as well as dramatically increasing Barracuda production and arguing to increase TSR production at the expense of RAF types. The Admiralty was still resistant to relying on US types at this point, partly because they believed the US would focus on types that were not suitable for escort carriers, and partly because they feared being left with little or nothing if the US decided to cut off supply, as had happened with the Martlet. The Admiralty's delegation in Washington was sceptical of these arguments and pushed for the acquisition of as many US aircraft as possible, while offering some scathing opinions on the quality of British aircraft. The Swordfish, the delegation felt,

> was obsolete in 1939 and will be ineffective as an operational aircraft in 1945. Apart from its complete lack of performance, armour and defensive fire, its range is so limited that it cannot be employed from first line carriers. Its poor take-off (with a depth charge or torpedo load) renders it unsuitable for world-wide operation from auxiliary carriers.[63]

The Fifth Sea Lord, Rear Admiral Denis Boyd, put up a qualified defence of the aircraft. "You say that the Swordfish is obsolete and this, of course, is perfectly true," he wrote,

> but it is having great success in the Battle of the Atlantic, and its peculiar qualities of slowness and ease of landing make it an extremely useful aircraft for operation in auxiliary carriers. Furthermore, it is easy to produce, and, for this particular type of operation, armed with RP [rocket projectiles], it is a formidable weapon and one which, already, the U-boats have cause to fear and dislike. It is noteworthy that the BOGUE* said they wished they had some Swordfish.[64]

In June, the Chief Naval Representative at the Ministry of Aircraft Production, Captain Matthew Slattery, said, "The Swordfish are now fitted with a free rocket take-off and are supreme."

---

*   USS *Bogue*, CVE-9, the first escort carrier to form a 'hunter-killer' group in the Atlantic.

11

DEFEATING THE U-BOATS

THE ALLIES were on the front foot in the Battle of the Atlantic by the summer of 1943 when convoy HS245 set out from Halifax to Liverpool with one of the biggest escorts yet assembled. The escort carrier, HMS *Chaser*, was carrying Avengers (which the Admiralty had finally recognised as a suitable type for the purpose) but the MAC ship *Empire Macalpine* was also there with her four Swordfish. At first, the weather was too rough for the lively *Chaser* to operate her newfangled monoplanes, while *Empire Macalpine*, with a hold full of grain, had a much steadier motion and once again the Swordfish held the line. On 1 July, however, the MAC ship was recovering aircraft, sailing across the path of the convoy and collided with the *Empire Ibex*, damaging the latter so severely she had to be abandoned with her load of beans, though the crew was taken off unharmed. *Empire Macalpine* seemed to have escaped without much damage, but the following day found that she was taking water in one of her holds, and although she was still capable of operating aircraft, it was decided that she would only do so in an emergency. She arrived in Liverpool with the convoy on 7 July.

When U-boat efforts were scaled back in the Atlantic after the failed spring offensive, it freed some escort carriers and their Swordfish for more offensive activities. In July 1943, *Archer* joined B5 Escort Group, a hunting group dispatched to take the fight to U-boats as they crossed the Bay of Biscay on their way to their operating areas. The experiment was compromised somewhat by operating within the range of Luftwaffe Fw 200s and Ju 88s, which put both carrier and aircraft at risk, and warned U-boats of their location. Though no U-boats were sunk, the exercise provided much useful learning and evidence that the 'hunter-killer' group could be a useful tactic against the U-boat threat in the right circumstances. *Archer*'s engines were in a worse state than ever though, so with new escort carriers and MAC ships starting to become available in numbers, the veteran was withdrawn for use as an accommodation ship.

HMS *Hunter*, now properly worked up after her earlier adventures on the Gibraltar run, took on the composite squadron 834 NAS and sailed for Gibraltar in August with *Stalker*, 833 Squadron aboard, in company. While on the way, she ran into a storm and all her aircraft were damaged in the hangar. She returned for replacement aircraft and headed back to the Mediterranean, disgorging a detachment of six Swordfish to North Front on the way, as did *Stalker*.

In the autumn of 1943, transatlantic convoys were well covered by escort carriers and MAC

The view from the rear cockpit of a Swordfish II from 835 Squadron as it takes off from HMS *Chaser* in November/December 1943.

ships, and while the returning U-boats brought new technology such as acoustic homing torpedoes, they once again failed to inflict severe losses, while losing nearly as many of their own number as ships sunk. One remaining area of the Atlantic that was not well covered by Allied forces was closed to U-boats by Operation *Alacrity*, establishing a base for long-range aircraft on the Azores. The Swordfish of 842 Squadron carried out anti-submarine patrols from Lagens airfield until the first RAF patrol aircraft were able to operate, returning on 24 October aboard *Fencer*.

After the Salerno landings of September 1943, *Battler* picked up 834 Squadron from Gibraltar and sailed through the Suez Canal into the Indian Ocean. After the defeat of the Atlantic U-boats in the spring, a wider autumn offensive was launched which included sending boats into the Indian Ocean where shipping was considered to be less well protected. This threatened supplies for the build-up of the Eastern Fleet, as it prepared to return to the East Indies and, eventually, the Pacific. *Battler* therefore escorted convoys sailing between Aden and Bombay from October, with the periods between convoys occupied with free-ranging hunts for blockade runners and U-boat supply ships.

It was not until March the following year that *Battler*'s crews finally reaped any concrete reward for their monotonous patrolling. One of

Anti-aircraft gunners of HMS *Battler* maintain a watch while 835 Squadron Swordfish are ranged aft.

A Swordfish II of 835 Squadron being brought up from the hangar of HMS *Battler* in 1943.

her Swordfish spotted the supply vessel *Brake* refuelling two U-boats and directed a destroyer to intercept. *Brake* was sunk, and one of the submarines was later detected and depth-charged by a Swordfish, without clear results though it did not menace the carrier again.

In late 1943, the threat from the wolfpacks had undoubtedly lessened, but in no small part that was down to the deterrence of heavy escorts on every convoy, and the pressure could not be taken off. By now, the build-up of forces in the UK ahead of the invasion of northern Europe was underway, and the convoys took on new meaning. They were no longer just a lifeline to keep the Allies from defeat, but a conduit for the final victory.

New ships and new weapons continued to join the fight. The antiquated Swordfish was yet again able to prolong its life as a platform for the latest technology, one example being the homing torpedo known as 'FIDO'. Ironically, one of these could have sunk an escort carrier during convoy HX265 when a Swordfish carrying one of these crashed astern of *Biter*. The impact released the torpedo, which fixed on the sound of the carrier's screw and struck the rudder, leaving it damaged but, fortunately, operable. A new radar would also become available: ASV Mk XI was capable of far greater precision than the earlier Mk II, although it was heavier than the earlier device, and had to be carried in a radome between the undercarriage legs, restricting offensive stores to the wings. Swordfish with the new radar were designated Mk III, and were delivered from February 1944.

In November that year, a new flight joined

Swordfish Mk III NR951, in July 1944. The ASV Mk XI radar was heavier and bulkier than the previous Mk II, so had to be located in tub between the undercarriage legs, ruling out use of a torpedo.

the MAC ship *Empire Macandrew*. Swordfish for the MAC ships were provided by 836 Squadron for British ships, and 860 Squadron for the two Dutch-registered vessels. The squadrons were based at Maydown in Northern Ireland, with separate flights being formed for each ship – 836H Flight was created in August 1943 and replaced 836M Flight after only one voyage aboard *Macandrew*. An observer with 836H was Sub-Lieutenant Brian Ryley who recalled the work with the MAC ship during this phase of the battle:

> We used to go across to Halifax, Nova Scotia, where we used to collect grain. And the grain, we used to put the grain in the hold, and then take it back to UK in a convoy, and we'd escort the convoy both ways, while we were at sea. If we could, because as you can imagine, the Atlantic isn't a very good place for a small ship in bad weather, and there were quite a few occasions when either we were caught out by the weather or we just couldn't fly because it was too bad. We used to do patrols around the convoy, and on occasions we were sent further afield to see if we could find any U-boats.

In the winter of 1943/4 in the North Atlantic, the MAC ship crews were fighting the conditions more than they were the enemy, and the discomfort of operating in an open-cockpit aircraft could

Aircraft of 860 (Dutch) Squadron at Maydown in County Londonderry in 1944. The squadron provided aircraft and crews for the two Dutch-owned MAC ships, *Gadila* and *Macoma*, and Maydown was its shore base.

be extreme. Even then, the crews never lost their affection for the Swordfish: "The Swordfish was an incredible aircraft really, considering its age and appearance. It did an awful lot of damage for an open biplane, a slow open biplane. Always respected it," Brian Ryley said.

> The only thing I didn't like about it, it was so bloody cold. Especially in the winter, in the North Atlantic. You literally had to dress in about two lots of clothes. We had flying suits, which weren't very warm, Irvin jackets and Irvin trousers as well, and also these long legged pants. We wore so much dress you could hardly move. The hardest part was blowing your nose, you used to wipe your nose on the sleeve of your Irvin jacket, which was a pretty dirty way of…

And it was not just the crew that was affected.

> In an open aircraft, open cockpit, and in the winter time it used to get very cold. On one occasion we were flying fairly near Iceland, and we came across a whole lot of pack ice in the sea. You'd expect the cold to make the engine colder, but it didn't, the oil in the engine went up to about a hundred and ten or something, because the oil was so thick, it wasn't moving through the cooler, and as a result it was warming up far more than it should do.

Fortunately, Ryley and his crew were able to return to the carrier before the engine failed.

Day flights would extend into night flights

if you got lost, which happened on one occasion. In fact we had one or two pilots who got lost and a previous crew to us, the pilot decided to head off for Iceland instead of trying to find the ship, but unfortunately he and the crew never reached Iceland. They were lost at sea. And on another occasion, I saw one of our Swordfish make a perfect landing on the MAC ship, and the next moment the ship gave a roll, and the next thing they were all in the sea. They got picked up. That happened all the time in the Atlantic.[65]

At this phase in the war, U-boat sightings were rare. The presence of escort carriers and MAC ships made the submarines wary, and while there were still sightings and attacks, many aircrews went through an entire posting on convoy duty without seeing a submarine. "We used to spot a few whales in the Atlantic which looked very similar to a U-boat," said Ryley. "Almost identical in fact, from the sky, which looked like sitting targets. But when we got down a bit lower they used to blow out their nose, and we'd realise it was a whale and not a U-boat."

Ryley and his crew, pilot Bob Meen and TAG Owen Cribb, sailed on four outbound and four homebound convoys with 836H Flight aboard *Empire Macandrew* between November 1943 and May 1944. By that time, the Atlantic convoys were all but secure. There were 19 MAC ships in operation by then, and they would start to be withdrawn from September that year. The focus of the war was already heading east. Ryley and his crew were transferred to 848 Squadron in Avengers and after a spell operating in support of the Normandy landings, embarked on HMS *Formidable* for service with the British Pacific Fleet.

By November 1943, the Admiralty's view that the Swordfish was the best type for anti-submarine warfare, expressed just a few months earlier, had been substantially revised. Seeing what the US Navy achieved in the Atlantic with its Avengers brought home to the last remaining Swordfish supporters that they had overstated its strengths and underestimated its weaknesses. That month, after conferring with the commander of a US Navy escort carrier, USS *Core*, the Commander-in-Chief, Western Approaches, wrote:

> The Avenger is a more suitable type of aircraft for antisubmarine work than the Swordfish. It has a stronger undercarriage, to stand up to rough weather landing. The Avenger's endurance of about 6 hours at a cruising speed of 150 knots gives about double the performance on one patrol of the Swordfish with a maximum endurance of 4 ½ hours at 90 knots. The maximum speed of the Avenger (240 knots) enables it to attack many U-boats which cannot be reached in time by the Swordfish with a maximum speed of about 130 knots. [He recommended that the FAA] Replace Swordfish by Tarpon aircraft at the first opportunity.[66]

A comparison of British and American escort carriers in the Atlantic revealed some stark truths. In the first 10 months of 1943, in comparable circumstances, USN carriers had sunk seven times the number of U-boats that their British counterparts had managed. Much of this was down to the different ways in which the services used their carriers in the Atlantic, with the USN being rather more freewheeling and offensive, but undoubtedly the aircraft played a substantial part too, in performance and reliability. "More than half the 65 casualties to British planes were cases of broken undercarriages and of crashes due to the plane bouncing on landing,"[67] wrote the Directorate of Naval Operational Studies. The casualty rate per sortie of the Swordfish was fully seven times that of the Avenger. US carrier aircraft converted 38% of sightings into kills while for British aircraft the

A Swordfish II of 816 Squadron is batted onto the flight deck of HMS *Tracker* in 1943. The ASV aerials have been removed by the censor. By 1943, the adoption of white on all but upper surfaces was becoming standard for Swordfish on escort carriers.

A Swordfish receives the cut from the batsman to land on a MAC ship. The narrowness of the deck, only 16ft 6in wider than a Swordfish's 45ft wingspan, is apparent.

The second British-built escort carrier, HMS *Activity*, with Swordfish ranged forward. *Activity*'s career started with deck-landing training in the Western Approaches area, and began work as a trade protection carrier in January 1944, with distant cover to two Gibraltar-bound convoys.

figure was only 17%. This was chiefly attributed to the Avenger's higher speed than the Swordfish. The report acknowledged that the Swordfish was still superior at night, as it was less visible (the Avenger's exhaust flame was very prominent in darkness), while the Swordfish had superior radar and greater manoeuvrability. However, it was noted that work was underway to address both issues on the Avenger.

In truth, the Fleet Air Arm had never had as many Avengers as it wanted, and in 1944 they were in far greater demand to equip strike squadrons on the RN's fleet carriers in the Far East. There was simply no alternative to keeping the Swordfish in service on some escort carriers – the MAC ships could not operate anything other than Swordfish, so the type that was meant to have been retired in the first year of the war in Europe found itself still in the front line as the war came to a close.

Even as the Battle of the Atlantic was winding down, convoys to Russia were experiencing a second crescendo. After the convoys were suspended in March 1943, they did not run again until November, and a carrier did not accompany them again until JW57 in February 1944. This was *Chaser*, with the Swordfish and Wildcats (as Martlets had been renamed) of 816 Squadron. Swordfish staggered into the air in the teeth of freezing gales in an effort to find U-boats, or just encourage them to keep their heads down.

The outward convoy reached Vaenga relatively unscathed and the escort joined the homeward

Three images showing the view from a Swordfish landing aboard HMS *Activity* in March 1943, first turning onto final approach, then coming in over the round-down 'at not more than 60 knots', and finally receiving the 'cut' from the batsman.

convoy RA57 on 2 March. Swordfish armed with RPs proved their worth again two days later when *Chaser*'s Swordfish 'B' found and attacked *U-472*, disabling her for a destroyer to finish off. Further attacks on U-boats were made, with the submarines possibly damaged each time. In the succeeding days two more U-boats were attacked with rockets and sunk, and others driven away.

The now-familiar deck accidents eroded *Chaser*'s stock of serviceable Swordfish to four, but she was able to keep patrols up. The convoy lost a merchantman and a destroyer to U-boats, but three U-boats had been sunk, two by aircraft alone and one by aircraft in concert with surface escorts.

Chaser had performed remarkably, but had been overstretched, so the next convoy would have two escort carriers. There was still no means of accelerating Swordfish off the deck in light winds as RATOG had still not been approved for use with the type. *Activity* and *Tracker* accompanied JW58 at the end of March, the latter with Avengers, and the former with only three Swordfish supplementing her seven Wildcats. While this convoy was working its way north, a powerful force of warships headed towards Norway and launched a carrier strike against the battleship *Tirpitz*, putting her out of action for three months. Swordfish had handed over their strike role, first to the Albacore and now to the Fairey Barracuda, but a number would still form part of Operation *Tungsten*, providing anti-submarine cover from *Furious* and *Fencer*. *Furious* and her Swordfish were well past their prime since their cruise off northern Norway back in 1940, but here they were still, refusing to lie down.

For the time being, the chief threat against the northern convoys would be U-boats and aircraft. JW58 continued, and on 3 April, one of *Activity*'s Swordfish, in concert with an Avenger and Wildcat from *Tracker*, attacked and blew up *U-288*.

The strong escort had defeated all U-boat attacks on JW58 and few attempts were made by U-boats to trouble RA58 on the way home. *Activity* became a fixture on the Russian run, with support from *Fencer* over the succeeding convoys, and through snowstorms and gales, they provided a robust defence against U-boats and aircraft alike, before convoys were suspended in May to support the Normandy landings.

The Russian convoys returned in August. Even at this late stage, new escort carriers were appearing, notably the British-built HMS *Nairana* and HMS *Campania*, which took part in their first convoys in January and June 1944 respectively,

On 1 May, HMS *Activity* was preparing to fly off the midday patrol of a rocket-armed Swordfish and two Martlets during convoy RA59 when a snowstorm engulfed the carrier as shown here. *Activity* was not properly 'Arcticised' so the commander was obliged to signal *Activity*'s counterpart, HMS *Fencer*, with the message "Will you please fly off this patrol as my flight deck is covered with snow?"

Late-production Mk III under test at Sherburn, in the last spec before production ended – 'hedgehog' exhaust, ASV Mk XI and rocket rails installed at the factory.

and both became regulars on the northern run. *Nairana* carried the mixed Swordfish/Sea Hurricane unit 835 Squadron, while *Campania*'s aircraft complement was provided by 813 Squadron with Swordfish, Wildcats and, on occasion, Fulmar night fighters. "We went on trips down to Gibraltar to start with. Three Gibraltar runs. And then it was Russian convoys. The first was on September '44," said Archie Hemsley, a sub-lieutenant pilot with 813 Squadron.

All the Swordfish were now Mk IIIs with the improved ASV Mk XI radar. Despite the highly challenging conditions and the small deck, Hemsley recalled that the aircraft still inspired confidence. Fortunately, by now, RATOG was finally available.

> A Swordfish is slow, so it was all right. Well when heavily loaded, we had RATOG, which are rockets. You pressed the button when you got to the end of the deck and then you didn't sink so much as you went towards the sea. You had to keep your hand jammed behind, here behind the throttle to stop pulling it back, as it pulled a lot of G. Nothing like a rocket to the moon, but there was quite a lot.[68]

The technological arms race between the Kriegsmarine and the Royal Navy had swung slightly in favour of the U-boats again. Notably, the 'Naxos' received enabled the Germans to detect ASV Mk XI emissions, so the crews had to be careful about using it. Hemlsey recalled:

> For example, we went out one night and got a radar reading. The Germans had a new H-radio pick-up mast, and we thought if we switched our radar off immediately, and then timed it to the spot, then we'd get

A Swordfish III of 836 Squadron taking off from the MAC ship *Empire McAndrew* (as indicated by the deck letters 'MK' on the forward end of the flight deck) with the aid of rocket-assisted take-off gear (RATOG).

it. Unfortunately, we didn't, they'd picked us up and it got away. You didn't have to sink them, you just had to be there. That's what did the trick. That's why the losses stopped on the Russian convoys.

Another new development, however, meant the Royal Navy was in a race against time to tackle the U-boats before it made a difference. "The point was that at the end, the Germans got the schnorkel," said Hemsley. Prior to this development,

> If you got the submarines down, then they couldn't race ahead of the convoy and catch it again. But with schnorkel they could. That was a mast that went up out of the sea and then they could run on diesel engines instead of batteries, and they could go at surface speed. In calm sea you could pick it up on the radar, but otherwise not. They were starting to come but not enough of them.[69]

One particular reason for pride in the Swordfish aboard *Campania* was that the very last of 2,392 aircraft constructed, was in their care. Swordfish NS204 had left the production line at Sherburn in August 1944, and a short ceremony was held to mark the end of an era. Captain H.C. Ranald, who was the MAP overseer at Blackburn, but also happened to have been the Commander Flying aboard HMS *Victorious* during the *Bismarck* chase, took the aircraft up for a brief flight before handing it over to the Air Transport Auxiliary for delivery to the navy. In October, NS204 was issued to 813 Squadron, where it was allocated to Acting Lieutenant Thomas Langley. Langley wrote to Blackburn in February 1945 asking for photographs of 'The Last of The Swordfish' for him and his crew, noting "as it is my own special aircraft I take great pride in it because it has done valuable work of late and has held the tradition of the remainder of its long line".[70]

That month, February 1945, *Campania* and *Nairana* escorted Operation *Hotbed*, the cover for JW64-RA64 to Kola Inlet and back. On the outward trip, relentless anti-submarine patrols were carried out by the exhausted Swordfish crews, with no sightings at all, only for a frigate to be torpedoed just as the convoy was entering Kola Inlet. As the return convoy was setting out, many U-boats were detected but the Swordfish failed to make contact and soon the weather made it all but impossible for both aircraft and submarines to operate. A Swordfish crashed over *Nairana*'s side as it attempted to land and the crew, virtually frozen after a few minutes in the water, were lucky to survive even with prompt action by the planeguard destroyer. *Nairana* undertook no more convoys but in March took part in an offensive sweep against enemy shipping off Norway in March. At the end of February, 813 Squadron left *Campania*, replaced by 825 Squadron of *Bismarck* and Channel Dash fame, which had previously been attached to HMS *Vindex*. With this unit aboard, *Campania* accompanied convoys JW65-RA65, the carrier's last operation.

The last Swordfish to be built, NS204, about to take its first flight at Sherburn in August 1944. A ceremony was held for factory staff, with Robert Blackburn and the Commander Flying of HMS *Victorious* during the *Bismarck* chase taking part, before the aircraft was handed over to the ATA for delivery to the navy.

Factory-fresh Swordfish Mk IIIs at Blackburn's Sherburn plant in early 1944, among the aircraft visible being NF301, NF302 and NF305.

Aircrew of 825 Squadron pose with one of the squadron's Swordfish aboard the escort carrier HMS *Vindex*, following the sinking of *Avenger* in September 1942.

12

DAY OF DAYS

WHEN PLANS for the invasion of France first began to be drawn up, the RAF was keen to see FAA involvement, even though carriers were ruled out at an early stage. In January 1944, Air Chief Marshal Sir Charles Portal, Chief of the Air Staff, made a request for 48 naval strike aircraft to support the invasion from land aerodromes, because of the FAA's expertise in anti-submarine and anti-surface vessel warfare. Coastal Command needed the assistance, being even more stretched than the Fleet Air Arm, and did not have the capacity to meet its ongoing commitments while protecting the invasion fleet from submarine and surface attack. Coastal Command was well aware of the capabilities of the Swordfish, having operated the odd squadron of the type itself, and 'borrowed' many more FAA units to operate from shore bases.

Coastal Command was aware that the Kriegsmarine, anticipating an invasion, was holding back large numbers of U-boats from Atlantic operations. It was imperative that anti-submarine squadrons were in place and trained to high efficiency.

Air Chief Marshal Sholto Douglas, Commander-in-Chief of Coastal Command, allotted the task of "The protection of our cross-channel convoys sailing along the South coast of England ... principally to the Fleet Air Arm Squadrons". These coastal convoys were situated principally between Lynmouth and Portland to the west, and between the Nore and Beachy Head to the east. The Fleet Air Arm Swordfish units were based at Perranporth in Cornwall (816), at Harrowbeer in Devon (838) and Manston in Kent (819), all arriving at their temporary bases in April.

One of the more unusual activities carried out by Fleet Air Arm squadrons was laying smoke screens to protect Allied shipping. The concentration of vulnerable shipping in and around the Channel required to allow the required, rapid build-up of forces in the beachhead posed real risks to the success of the operation. No fewer than eight convoys were due to arrive on the day following the initial landings, some of which were required to pass through the narrows at the Strait of Dover, which were covered by heavy gun batteries, and provided a 'pinch-point' where E-boats could wreak havoc. One means of safeguarding the convoys was to cover the passage of the convoy with smoke screens—a tactic familiar to the RN for use in naval battles.

It was intended that the smoke would be laid by motor launches (MLs), but there were insufficient launches equipped for this role to cover convoy ETP1—the first attempt to pass large troopships through the strait for four years. Admiral Ramsay,

A Swordfish landing on 'Project Lily' a floating airstrip constructed of connected flotation units (which had been developed for Mulberry harbours) with a runway formed of metal strips over the top. A Swordfish Mk III with RATOG was one of two aircraft to take part in assessments in the Firth of Clyde.

in command of Operation *Neptune*, the naval component of the invasion, noted that "arrangements were made with Coastal Command for FAA aircraft to assist MLs in laying smoke screens for this and other convoys". After some difficulties were encountered, Ramsay noted that "A most effective smoke screen … was finally laid and convoy ETP1 passed through the Straits at 1700, 6th June, without any enemy interference". The aircraft laying the smoke screen on this occasion were the Swordfish of 819 Squadron, commencing at 1518 and maintained as long as necessary. As Ramsay noted, smoke-laying by naval Swordfish was employed for future convoys.

On 6 June when *Overlord* was launched, large numbers of U-boats left their Atlantic bases and headed for the Channel; Coastal Command sighted 36 off the mouth of the English Channel in the four days after the invasion began. As mentioned, most of the submarines heading for the invasion area were fitted with schnorkels, breathing devices that allowed them to operate their diesel engines while submerged, making them hard to spot both visually and with ASV. For the rest of the month, 47 sightings were made, more than half of them resulting in attacks.

Emblazoned with 'invasion stripes,' this Swordfish of 816 Squadron, Perranporth, was part of the Fleet Air Arm's direct contribution to D-Day, carrying out coastal patrols, day and night, in case of U-boat and torpedo boat efforts to undermine the invasion.

Light surface forces, meanwhile, were pitted against the invasion fleet in large numbers. Admiral Ramsay noted that "Throughout the month of May enemy E-Boat activity in the Central Channel increased, and it was apparent that more E-boats were being moved to Cherbourg and Havre." Sholto Douglas added, "The operations of Coastal Command against these light forces consisted mainly of continuous anti-shipping patrols in the Channel. Albacores, Avengers, Swordfish, Beaufighters and Wellingtons made a great many attacks, mainly at night, against E-boats, R-boats, 'M'-class minesweepers and trawlers." He added, "We know from prisoners of war that hardly an E-boat put to sea without being spotted and attacked from the air … there is no doubt that the menace of the enemy's light forces was held in check."

By August, the need for Fleet Air Arm squadrons supporting the Channel operations lessened — 816 NAS disbanded, while 838 NAS decamped to Northern Ireland to help cover the Western Approaches. Only 819 Squadron continued, taking its Swordfish to Knokke-le-Zoute in Belgium to tackle shipping off the Dutch coast along with the RAF's 119 Squadron. The latter unit had been one of

Swordfish Mk III NF410 'NH-F' of 119 Squadron RAF based at Knokke in Belgium for night anti-shipping operations against German forces operating in the Channel in early 1945. This aircraft is armed with 250lb bombs and parachute flares.

a few RAF squadrons using naval types on coastal anti-shipping operations. It was equipped exclusively with the Albacore until February 1945, when, in an unusual move, it began to re-equip with the older type — though in truth, the Swordfish Mk IIIs were mostly newer airframes than the more modern Albacores.

The squadron's first operational patrol with a Swordfish took place on 6 February, with a couple more over the succeeding days mixed with Albacore sorties, until the 11th when all patrols were carried out with Swordfish. The chief occupation for 819 and 119 Squadrons at this time was patrolling for Biber miniature submarines, which were operating out of the Scheldt, and E-boats attempting to hamper cross-Channel shipping.

In February, 819 Squadron returned to Bircham Newton and disbanded the following month, leaving 119 Squadron to maintain the Swordfish's presence. The patrols could be as monotonous as the Atlantic equivalent, and an entry in the squadron's diary on 22 February referred to "patrols which proved to be uneventful (how cheesed we are getting with that word!)".[71] Night and day patrols were carried out, mostly without incident and often frustrating. Occasional radar blips failed to lead to anything concrete, and once when a strong contact was tracked, the crew had to bomb blind using the radar as mist blocked all visibility.

On 11 March, however, two Bibers were spotted by Flight Lieutenant Campbell flying the Anson communications aircraft, who managed to sink one simply by 'buzzing' it, causing the crew to abandon ship and scuttle their craft. On his return,

A formation of 119 Squadron's distinctive black Swordfish over the Channel in early 1945. The Swordfish replaced Albacores in February.

two Swordfish was immediately dispatched to search for the other Biber. This was spotted surfacing, and a determined depth charge attack led to a probably sinking, and "a great deal of tail-wagging in the mess that night".[72] Campbell was nicknamed 'Killer' as a result of his exploits. The following day saw more success with two groups of fast motor boats believed to be 'Linsen' suicide boats. One was disabled with depth charges despite this being a rather unsuitable weapon, and Tempests were called up to deal with the remaining boats. Later in the day, two more Bibers were spotted, attacked and claimed sunk. "Four Bibers in two days! Whizzo!" recorded the squadron diary.

Another attack was made on 12 April, when Petty Officer Goundry surprised two Bibers surfacing next to each other and dropped a stick of bombs between them. He reported that the first was "blown out of the water and left stationary on the surface" and that "The second was not seen again."

The squadron continued operating from Knokke, Manston and Bircham Newton until VE Day. One Swordfish marked the occasion by flying low over a group of German prisoners. The navigator leaned out of the cockpit, patted the side of his trusty aircraft, and shouted "Look what beat you, you ******s."

Some Swordfish went east as the Royal Navy

Swordfish II LS454 of 733 Squadron fleet requirements unit at RN Aircraft Maintenance Yard, Clappenburg Bay, Ceylon in 1945. It wears Eastern Fleet markings and all-over aluminium dope. The aircraft next to it are Boulton-Paul Defiants.

did, but in strictly non-operational roles. With the end of the war, the elderly biplane was now almost completely surplus to requirements, and most airframes were well used, but peace was not quite the end for the type's military service.

A couple were adopted by station flights attached to Royal Navy shore establishments as hacks. Six redundant Swordfish were spotted assembled near the repair yard at RNAS Donibristle (HMS *Merlin*) in 1946. The six airframes went into the hangar and emerged as two flyable examples — NF389 and NF399.[73]

Meanwhile, development of torpedoes continued, and in the Swordfish, the Air Torpedo Development Unit at Gosport had found the perfect platform for low-speed drops of experimental torpedoes. A handful of Swordfish were operated by this unit from shortly before the end of the war until 1951, when NF399 was written off after a landing accident. This was the last Swordfish to be scrapped. NF389 continued as a hack and display aircraft, at the time the last Swordfish on Royal Navy charge, with 781 Squadron based at Lee-on-Solent.

Fairey had recognised the importance of saving a Swordfish for posterity shortly after the end of the war, and as there were no more Fairey-built examples around, the company obtained LS326 from Sherburn in 1946, and later painted it in Fairey house colours of blue and silver. Both this aircraft and NF389 were borrowed by 20th Century Fox for the filming of *Sink the Bismarck!* in 1959, where they received camouflage schemes and the codes 5A and 5B respectively, which they both wore for some years afterwards. NF389 was withdrawn from flight during the 1960s, while LS326 was eventually donated to the Royal Navy and was a founding aircraft in the Royal Navy Historic Flight (RNHF) in 1972.

Eleven Swordfish are known to survive as of

Swordfish Mk II NF399 '912' in postwar Extra Dark Sea Grey over Sky markings, during its time with the Station Flight RNAS Arbroath in 1948, before joining the Air Torpedo Development Unit (ATDU) at Gosport later that year.

2022. Seven of these were preserved after being acquired after the war by collector Ernie Simmons in Canada and stored on his farm, all but one being auctioned off in 1970. The exception was Mk I W5856 which was sold in the 1950s to a company that intended to use it for crop-dusting, then acquired by the now-defunct Strathallan collection and brought to the UK, eventually going to the RNHF and being returned to flight.

HS544, another Simmons aircraft, was restored to flight by Bob Spence and flown in Canada for many years before returning to Britain in 2019, to be based at White Waltham, where LS326 had operated in the late 1940s and 1950s. NF389 was also passed to the RNHF, and was employed as a static display at airshows for a period before being used as a spares source for the two flying aircraft. Navy Wings, which now operates the RNHF aircraft on the civil register, has aspirations to restore NF389 to join W5856 and LS326 when resources allow. In years to come, it is not beyond the realms of possibility that three or even four flying Swordfish might be seen in UK skies for the first time since the ATDU's operations shortly after the war

Mk II NF389 in late 1940s FAA colour scheme in the late 1940s. A Barracuda Mk V can be seen in the background. NF389 was one of a number of Swordfish operated by the ATDU in the late 1940s and early 1950s, but the only one retained by the Royal Navy.

Fairey Swordfish NR933 at Culham in 1949. This was another of the ATDU Swordfish which was lost in October 1950 when the pilot reported difficulties during a flight from Culdrose to the test range at the Isles of Scilly. The Swordfish ditched but despite a search, no trace was found. Flight Lieutenant E.B. Churchill's body was not recovered.

Fairey Swordfish NF389 and a Westland Wyvern VZ733 in July 1953 – "The Navy's only remaining 'Stringbag'" – demonstrating how far carrier-based torpedo bombers had come in less than two decades.

Fairey Aviation's Swordfish Mk II, the former LS326, a former MAC ship aircraft, after receiving the civil registration G-AJVH, which it carried from 1946 until it was presented back to the Navy in 1960. G-AJVH was reconditioned in 1955 and painted in Fairey house colours of blue and silver.

NOTES

1. Ian M. Philpott, *The Royal Air Force: Re-Armament 1930 to 1939*, Barnsley: Pen & Sword, 2006, p. 434
2. H.A. Taylor, *Fairey Aircraft since 1915*, London: Putnam & Co., 1974, p. 18
3. Requirements for aircraft carriers, Memorandum by Director of Plans, 24 January 1940, ADM 1/11971
4. Order for Fairey Swordfish instead of Fairey Albacores, Treasury Inter-Service Committee Fleet Air Arm, 25 October 1939, ADM 1/10114
5. Requirements for aircraft carriers, Memorandum by Director of Plans, 24 January 1940, ADM 1/11971
6. Ibid
7. Report of Proceedings from Commanding Officer HMS Furious to Vice Admiral Commanding Battlecruiser Squadron, 30 April 1940, ADM 199/479
8. Ibid
9. Ibid
10. Operation DX – Report by the Vice Admiral Aircraft Carriers, 15 June 1940, ADM 199/479
11. Letter from Commander-in-Chief Home Fleet to Secretary of the Admiralty, 14 May 1940, ADM 199/479
12. Operation DX – Report by the Vice Admiral Aircraft Carriers, 15 June 1940, ADM 199/479
13. H.A. Taylor, *Fairey Aircraft since 1915*, London: Putnam & Co., 1974, p. 249
14. John Jordan & Robert Dumas, *French Battleships 1922–1956*, Annapolis, MD: Naval Institute Press, 2009, p. 85
15. John Sutherland m& Diane Canwell, *Vichy Air Force at War: The French Air Force that Fought the Allies in World War II*, Barnsley: Pen & Sword, 2011, p. 23
16. Admiral Sir A.B. Cunningham, Report of an action with the Italian Fleet off Calabria 9 July 1940, *Supplement to The London Gazette*, 27 April 1948, pp. 2643–4
17. Ugolino Vivaldi, parte 1, Con la pelle appesa a un chiodo website https://conlapelleappesaaunchiodo.blogspot.com/2020/03/ugolino-vivaldi-parte-1.html
18. John Wellham, *With Naval Wings: The Autobiography of a Fleet Air Arm Pilot in World War II*, Staplehurst: Spellmount, p. 65
19. Ibid
20. Report from Commanding Officer HMS Ark Royal to Secretary of the Admiralty, ADM 199/446, 3 August 1940
21. Ibid
22. Angelo N. Caravaggio, 'The Attack at Taranto', *Naval War College Review* Vol. 59: No. 3, 2006
23. Letter from Commander-in-Chief Mediterranean to Secretary of Admiralty, 16 January 1941, ADM 199/167
24. John Wellham, *With Naval Wings: The Autobiography of a Fleet Air Arm Pilot in World War II*, Staplehurst: Spellmount, p. 79
25. Letter from Commander-in-Chief Mediterranean to Secretary of Admiralty, 16 January 1941, ADM 199/167

26 Angelo N. Caravaggio, 'The Attack at Taranto', *Naval War College Review* Vol. 59: No. 3, 2006
27 Condition of Swordfish aircraft of 821 Squadron 'X' Flight received to reinforce Malta, Report from CO HMS Ark Royal to Flag Officer commanding Force H, 16 January 1941, ADM 1/11148
28 John Wellham, *With Naval Wings: The Autobiography of a Fleet Air Arm Pilot in World War II*, Staplehurst: Spellmount, pp. 120–1
29 Ibid. p. 123
30 War Diary, 24–30 April 1941, Document 204 in Michael Simpson (ed.) *The Cunningham Papers*, Vol. 1, Ashgate and Naval Records Society, 1999, p. 368
31 Report from Commanding Officer HMS Formidable to Rear-Admiral Mediterranean Aircraft Carriers, 10 April 1941, ADM 199/781
32 Ibid
33 Threat posed by Bismarck and Graf Zeppelin, Minute by Director of Plans, 29 January 1940, ADM 1/10617
34 Details from: Report from Commanding Officer HMS Victorious to Commander-in-Chief Home Fleet, 28 May 1941, ADM 199/1187
35 Mark E. Horan, *With Gallantry and Determination: The Story of the Torpedoing of the Bismarck*, Copyright 1998–2019 KBismarck.com
36 Extract from Dispatch from Commander-in-Chief Home Fleet to Secretary of the Admiralty, 5 July 1941, ADM 199/1187
37 See Uboat.net website, 'HMS Victorious (38): Aircraft Carrier of the Illustrious-class' page, https://uboat.net/allies/warships/ship/3259.html
38 Report from Commanding Officer HMS Ark Royal to Secretary of Admiralty: Torpedo attack on Bismarck, 6 June 1941, ADM 199/1187
39 Ibid
40 'Ark Royal Planes – Cork Forest Set on Fire', *Canberra Times*, 28 August 1941, p. 2
41 Loss of HMS Courageous 17 September 1939, Letter from the Commander-in-Chief Western Approaches to the Secretary of the Admiralty, 15 October 1939, ADM 156/195
42 'Channel Dash – The Bravest of the Brave', History of Manston Airfield website: www.manstonhistory.org.uk/channel-dash-bravest-brave/
43 Ibid
44 Recommendation for Decoration or Mention in Dispatches, Eugene R. Esmonde, 825 Squadron, FAA RN Air Station Lee-on-[the-]Solent, 17 February 1942, ADM 1/2460
45 Defensive Strategy in Indian Ocean, Message from Commander-in-Chief Eastern Fleet to Admiralty, 2 May 1942, PREM 3/171/4
46 Commander Bertie W. Vigrass OBE VRD, 'To Sea in A Barracuda', Letter to the author, 30 January 2013
47 Minutes by Director of Naval Air Division of Meeting Held at Admiralty on 12 December 1940, 14 December 1940, ADM 1/11139
48 Supply of Grumman Martlet Fighters, Minute from the First Lord of Admiralty to Prime Minister, 6 December 1941, AVIA 46/136
49 Kenneth Poolman, *Escort Carrier 1941–1945: An Account of British Escort Carriers in Trade Protection*, London: Ian Allen ,1972, p. 24
50 Interim report from Commanding Officer 812 Squadron to Commanding Officer HMS Argus, 17 January 1942, IWM 78/1/1]
51 Aircraft requirements in 1944, Minute by Director of Naval Air Division, 15 February 1942, ADM 1/11938
52 Minute by Head of Air Branch, Orders for Fairey Swordfish aircraft for Auxiliary Carriers, 4 April 1942, ADM 1/11956
53 Ibid. p. 49
54 Ibid. p. 49
55 Minute from First Lord of Admiralty to Prime Minister, Development of Fleet Air Arm, 27 October 1942, ADM 205/14
56 Report of Enquiry by Director of Naval Construction, Loss of HMS *Avenger*, 4 January 1943, ADM 1/12605
57 Notes by Military Branch of meeting held by Assistant Chief of Naval Staff, Allocation and employment of escort carriers, 17 February 1943, ADM 1/13642
58 George John Humphreys, Imperial War Museum Oral history, Catalogue Number 33568, Reel 3, www.iwm.org.uk/collections/item/object/80032553
59 Peter Jinks interviewed by the author, Navy Wings Swordfish Heritage Day, RNAS Yeovilton, 21

September 2018
60 Sinking of U-752, 819 Squadron Diary, 23 May 1943, ADM 207/15
61 Report of Proceedings from Commanding Officer, HMS Biter, to Commander-in-Chief Western Approaches, 3 May 1943, ADM 237/112
62 Brian Ryley in conversation with the author, 11 August 2020
63 'Aircraft production and policy', Letter from Head of British Admiralty Delegation Washington to Secretary of Admiralty, 4 March 1943, ADM 1/13485
64 Letter from Fifth Sea Lord to Head of British Admiralty Delegation, Washington, 'Comments on Head of British Admiralty Delegation's letter of 4 March, 11 June 1943', ADM 1/13485
65 Brian Ryley in conversation with the author, 16 March and 20 August 2020
66 'Employment of British and American Escort Carriers in Anti-U-boat Warfare', Letter from Commander-in-Chief Western Approaches to Secretary of Admiralty, 7 November 1943, ADM 1/12865
67 Achievements of British and American Escort Carriers in Antisubmarine Operations 1943, Report No. 9/44 by Directorate of Naval Operational Studies, 12 February 1944, ADM 219/95
68 Archie Hemsley interviewed by the author, Navy Wings Swordfish Heritage Day, RNAS Yeovilton, 21 September 2018
69 Ibid
70 Acting Lieutenant Thomas Langley, Letter to Blackburn Aircraft, 27 February 1943, BAE Systems Brough Heritage archive
71 Operations Record Book 119 Squadron RAF, February 1945, AIR 27/910/36
72 Operations Record Book 119 Squadron RAF, March 1945, AIR 27/910/38
73 *Navy News*, May 1999, p. 6

DATA

(Mk I unless otherwise stated)
Span: 45.5ft (13.87m)
Length: 40ft (12.19m)
Height: 16ft (4.88m)
Wing area: 549 sq ft (51 sq m)
Max weight: 9,100lb (4,128kg)
Standard weight: 7,500lb (3,402kg)
Tare weight: 4,700lb (2,132kg)
Max speed: 138mph (222km/h) at 5,000ft (1,524m)
Max speed Mk II: 143mph (230 km/h) at 4,750ft (1,448m)
Max speed Mk III: 131mph (211 km/h) at 4,750ft (1,448m)
Powerplant: Bristol Pegasus IIIM.3 630hp
Powerplant Mk II/III: Bristol Pegasus 30 750hp
Fuel capacity: 167gal (759l)
Max endurance: 5.65 hours
Range: 875 miles (1,408km)
Guns: 1 x .303in forward-facing, 1 x .303in flexible mount
Ordnance: 1 x 1,500lb torpedo or mine (except Mk III), 3 x 250lb depth charges, 8 x rocket projectiles, 2 x 500lb bombs

INDEX

Aeroplane and Armament Experimental Establishment (A&AEE) 12, 14, 93, 94
Augusta, raids on 38, 44, 45, 49

Blackburn Aircraft Company 7–9, 11, 12, 14, 19, 21, 25, 27, 30, 59, 86, 88, 112, 113
Bridge, Capt A.M. (Captain, *Eagle*) 44, 46
Burch, Capt A.R. RM 32

Cagliari, raids on 47, 51
Calabria, Battle of 41, 44, 45, 54
Campioni, V-Adm Inigo 43, 54, 55, 60
Cape Spartivento, Battle of 47, 54
convoys 29, 38, 41, 43, 44, 51, 54, 57, 59, 60, 65, 72, 73, 80, 83, 84, 86–90, 92–8, 100, 101, 103, 104, 106, 108–12, 115, 116
Cunningham, V-Adm Andrew 38, 43, 44, 45, 49, 52, 54, 58, 60, 61

Duplex pistol (torpedo) 54, 61, 63, 68

Esmonde, Lt-Cdr E.R. 65, 66, 74, 75

Forbes, Adm Sir Charles 36, 45
Force H 38, 40, 47, 49, 54, 55, 57, 65, 67, 69, 73

Iachino, Adm Angelo 60, 61, 73

Lily, Project 116

MAC ship 90, 91, 98–100, 104–8, 112, 123
Menzies, Duncan (test pilot) 12–15
Moffatt, Sub-Lt J.W.C. 'Jock' 70

Narvik, 1940 battles of 31–3, 36
Navy Wings 121

Operations
    Alacrity 101
    Catapult 39, 40
    Collar 54
    Crush 47
    DX 34
    DW 31
    Fuller ('Channel Dash') 74, 87, 112
    Halberd 73
    Hats 49
    Hurry 47
    Ironclad (invasion of Madagascar) 78
    Judgement (Battle of Taranto) 51–4, 56, 62, 68
    MB3 49
    MB6 50
    MB8 51, 53, 54
    Menace 47, 49, 60, 103, 117
    Mincemeat (1941 raid on Sardinia) 72, 73
    Neptune (Normandy landings, naval) 116

INDEX

Result 57
Substance **72**
Weserübung 29

Patch, Capt 'Ollie' RM 45
Pound, Adm Sir Dudley 74

Red Sea Flotilla 59, 60
Rice, PO F.C. 31, 32, 61
Royal Navy Historic Flight 120

ships
   Bruno Heinemann 30
   Admiral Hipper 29, 30
   Adolph Woermann 27
   Andromeda 60
   Bismarck 65–74, 112, 113, 120
   Caio Duilio 57
   Cesare Battista 59
   Conte di Cavour 52, 53
   Daniele Manin 59
   Dunkerque 40, 41
   Empire Ibex 100
   Empire Macalpine 98, 100
   Empire Macandrew 99, 104, 106
   Friedrich Eckoldt 30
   Giovanni Acerbi 59
   Gneisenau 36, 74, 75
   Graf Spee 27, 28
   Guilio Cesare 43, 53, 59
   HMS *Activity* 89, 90, 108–10
   HMS *Archer* 84, 86, 90, 92–94, 96, 97, 100
   HMS *Argus* 27, 38, 47, 56
   HMS *Ark Royal* 21, 24–29, 31, 32, 34, 36, 38, 40, 41 46, 47, 49, 51, 54–57, 65, 67, 69–74, 83, 87
   HMS *Attacker* 88
   HMS *Audacity* 81, 83, 84, 86
   HMS *Avenger* 84, 87–90, 97, 100, 106, 108, 109, 114, 117
   HMS *Biter* 97–89, 93–97, 103
   HMS *Black Swan* 34
   HMS *Campania* 109, 111, 112
   HMS *Chaser* 100, 101, 108, 109
   HMS *Courageous* 12, *24, 25, 27, 38*
   HMS *Eagle* 27, 29, 38, 39, 41–46, 49, 50, 52, 59, 60, 71–3
   HMS *Formidable* 21, 59–64, 72, 77, 78, 106
   HMS *Furious* 23, 27, 29–34, 109
   HMS *Glorious* 15, 18, 22, *24, 25, 27, 28,* 31, 34, 36, 38, 52
   HMS *Hermes* 27, 29, 40, 41, 77
   HMS *Illustrious* 21, 49–53, 56
   HMS *Nairana* 109, 111, 112
   HMS *Renown* 27, 57
   HMS *Resolution* 32
   HMS *Stalker* 97, 100
   HMS *Tracker* 107, 109
   HMS *Vindex* 112, 114
   HMS *Warspite* 27, 31–3, 43, 61
   Ingo 58
   Leone Pancaldo 44
   Littorio 52-54
   Nazario Sauro 59
   Pantera 59, 60
   Paul Jacobi 30, 31
   Po 60
   Pola 61
   Rapana 98
   Richelieu 41, 47, 49
   Santa Maria 60
   Saint Didier 63
   Scharnhorst 36, 55, 74
   Strasbourg 27, 40
   Theodor Riedel 30
   Tigre 59
   Trento 53
   Ugolino Vivaldi 44
   USS *Bogue* 99fn
   USS *Coreb* 106
   Vittorio *Veneto* 52, 53, 55, 61
shore stations
   Crail 30
   Dekheila 15, 41, 50, 56, 64, 72
   Donibristle 120
   Evanton 29, 34
   Gosport 20, 41, 120, 121

Hal Far 15, 19, 38, 56, 58
Hatston 29, 36, 55
Knokke-le-Zoute 117-119
Lee-on-the-Solent 35, 74, 120
Manston 74, 115, 119
Maydown 104, 105
Somerville, Adm Sir James 38, 40, 54–6, 73, 77
squadrons (Fleet Air Arm unless otherwise stated)
   3 AACU (RAF) 49
   119 (RAF) 117-19
   767 38, 39
   810 21, 26, 27, 34, 40, 47, 51, 55, 68, 73, 79, 80
   811 15, 24, 81, 94
   812 15, 17, 22, 24, 34, 36, 73, 83, 84
   813 38, 41, 43–6, 50, 59, 73, 91, 111, 112
   814 41, 77
   816 30, 31, 73, 87, 92, 107, 108, 115, 117
   818 30, 31, 40, 51, 67, 68, 70
   820 21, 28, 29, 34, 40, 47, 51, 67–9
   821/821X 21, 27, 34, 36, 55, 72
   823 22, 34, 36
   825 15, 18, 19, 24, 34, 36, 65, 66, 73–5, 87, 89, 112, 114
   826 59, 60, 63, 64, 72
   829 59, 60, 63, 64, 78–80
   830 38, 49, 55–8, 72, 80
   833 89, 100
   834 86, 100, 101
   835 88, 101–3, 111
   836 87, 99, 104, 112
   860 (Dutch) 91, 104, 105
Staniland, Chris (Fairey test pilot) 10, 11

Taranto, Battle of 51–4, 56, 62, 68
Tobruk 41, 45, 50
Troubridge, Capt T.H. 31, 33

U-boats 24, 25, 27, 36, 73, 80, 83, 84, 86, 87, 89, 92–7, 99–101, 103, 104, 106–9, 111, 112, 115–17

Vigrass, Bertie OBE 78, 79

Wellham, Lt John 45, 46, 52, 53, 59, 71
Wells, V-Adm Lionel 34, 40
Western Approaches 24, 27, 83, 106, 108, 117